T0193874

OUR MOTHER'S TEARS:
A Book About Gangs

Manuel Jaramillo

 www.trafford.com

North America & international
toll-free: 1 888 232 4444 (USA & Canada)
phone: 250 383 6864 ♦ fax: 812 355 4082

CONTENTS

A Book About Gangs

Lagrimas de Nuestra Madres

Our Mothers' Tears

A mother's grief . . .
Is beyond belief.
She just sits and cries . . .
As you live with lies.
©©©
But what can a mother do . . .
To take away the blues?
As she watches you fade away . . .
Losing a part of you every single day.
©©©
Will you wipe away her tears?
And put to rest her fears?
Or will you do what she feels you will?
Pick up a gun and kill!
©©©
She cuddled you at birth . . .
Loved you for all you're worth.
And now you're tearing her apart . . .
As you slowly break her heart!
©©©
A mother's love can never be replaced . . .
And the memory of you can never be erased.
Her life goes on in agony and pain . . .
For without you, it'll never be the same!

INTRODUCTION

A MOTHER'S GRIEF

I'm sure that all of us love our mothers. That pretty much goes without saying. However, most of us take them for granted. We unintentionally do not appreciate our mothers or what we put them through when we take the twists and turns of our lives. We forget that their hearts can be broken by our actions, and we don't understand the ramifications of our actions relative to them. Mothers are our nurturers and the ones who raise us more intimately, so their attachment to us is even that much more significant than we may assume it is. Mothers love us, mothers cry over us, and mothers worry over us. It's just what they do, and when we do things that put us in harm's way, become drunks or drug addicts, put ourselves in jail or prison, we don't realize just how those things affect them. This is especially true when we get involved in gangs and develop associations with those who are involved with gangs.

I know that I am personally responsible for the majority of heartache and sadness that my mother experienced in her life. I was her baby (don't they all have one?) and I was probably her biggest cause for concern of the four of us she raised. I was always the one who got into trouble at home and with law enforcement. I was the one who rebelled at home and stood up to the man who helped raise me. I was the one who started smoking early and testing out the local drugs. I was the one who skipped school just to go get into trouble. And ultimately, I was the one who was taken away at an early age and out into a reformatory for incorrigible youths.

On top of all of that, she had to experience the fear and trepidation of my being in the midst of one of the most violent prison riots in

American history (the riot in the New Mexico State Penitentiary in Santa Fe, N.M.) when I was still pretty much a young teen. She worried for three days without knowing whether or not I had survived, as the devastation that occurred in the first three days of that riot did not allow for an accounting of inmates in a factual manner. She actually found my name on a list printed in the Albuquerque Journal newspaper of inmates (including myself) who had made it out to the prison yard and given their identity to prison officials, for the sake of notifying loved ones.

She was terrified when I was stabbed in the Administrative Segregation Yard of a Northern California prison by members of a rival prison gang. It brought back memories of her worries over Santa Fe. I choose not to relate the details of this assault as it might identify who I am to those who may be looking for retribution. And when I was branded as one of the worst prison inmates in the California Department of Corrections and Rehabilitation, it caused her much worry, as I was validated as a prison gang member of the Nuestra Raza/Nuestra Familia prison gang and sent to the Security Housing Unit at Pelican Bay State Prison in where I remained in total isolation for several years. I would once again find myself at the S.H.U. in later years. This time I was sent to the Corcoran State Prison Security Housing Unit where I was once again isolated for the next three years.

For several decades, I have caused my mother undue hardship, care, and concern. She has helped me out financially and kept in touch with me throughout the years (20 plus years), in hopes of getting me to see the folly of my ways. Well, mother, I finally have. I disassociated myself from my gang ties and have left that life to become a normal productive human being. I am free from the oppression of the gang culture and the bonds that kept me down and in and out of prison for most of my life.

And so, I write this book both for myself as a healing process, and for those who are continually at risk, or in the midst of their own dilemma. I strongly urge you to free yourselves of that burden for it has no rewards . . . only penalties. Please read my book and enlighten yourselves to the brutal truth about gangs and gang membership. Take a serious reality check my young brothers before you lose. And to those of who have loved ones on the peripheral edges of the gang culture, take heed and glean what you can from this book so that it may help you help them. Save somebody's life!

For this reason, I dedicate this book to the mothers who have lost children to gang violence and continue to suffer. And I offer a prayer to our Lord in Heaven that your sons, your brothers, your fathers, and uncles too, will open their eyes to the error of life that they are living in and get out before they pay the ultimate price, life in the S.H.U. going nowhere fast; on death row going to that final room; or dead at the hands of another gang member. Furthermore, that each of your mothers' prayers will be answered in relation to their lost sons, that they may soon find their way. God loves us all, and all we need to do to gain his full love is to accept him in our hearts and believe that Jesus Christ is our Lord and Savior, and do his will.

I write this book under an assumed name so as not to endanger myself and my family from retribution by those still actively participating in La Nuestra Raza/Nuestra Familia Prison Gang. I know the inner workings of the organization and how they operate and am always wary of possible repercussions for my actions (dropping out and debriefing) and for writing this "truth be told book," for I know that to expose their agenda as I have, as well as the agendas of California's other formidable prison gangs would bring about serious retribution upon myself and my family, should my true identity be discovered.

Every other book I have seen written on this topic has been a self-serving glorification of gang life, and all the lethal intricacies involved in that life are left hidden from the reader's eye. They want you to think that being a gang member is something special and glorious, when, in reality, that couldn't be further from the truth. I speak the gut truth about the realities of gang life. Gangsters live by the sword and they also die by the sword if they continue in their ways. Help me to help you by reading this book thoroughly.

Mama doesn't sleep well at night . . .
For your actions give her fright.
Every time she hears the phone ring . . .
She dreads the news that it may bring.
©©©
Of her wayward son's cruel demise.
Knowing one day soon, he'll pay the price.
She prays to God for intervention . . .
And sometimes wishes for his detention.
©©©
At least that way he'll stay alive . . .
She knows no other way that he'll survive.
The tears keep running from her eyes . . .
As she sees right through all of his lies.
©©©
Wishing her little boy would just come on home . . .
Back to mama where he belongs.
He's living life way too fast . . .
At this pace he will not last.
©©©
One day soon he will be gone . . .
Without a chance to say so long.
What is mama supposed to do?
For her life is over without you!
©©©
She runs around, her nerves well frayed . . .
Waiting to hear that her son got played.
Is this what she deserves?
Her wayward son's wretched curse.

A Book About Gangs

Manuel Jaramillo

CHAPTER ONE

The history of gangs

Gangs:
"A set of implements or devices arranged to operate together; a group of persons working together; especially a group of criminals or young delinquents. To attack in a gang; to form into or move or act as a gang."

A **gang** is a group of people, through the organization, formation, and establishment of an assemblage, share a common identity. Its contemporary meaning typically denotes a criminal organization or else a criminal affiliation. In early usage, the word gang referred to a group of workmen. In the United Kingdom, the word is still often used in this sense, but it later underwent a lessening of its meaning. The word gang often carries a negative connotation; however, within a gang which defines its self in opposition to mainstream norms, members may adopt the phrase as a statement of identity or defiance.

The California Department of Corrections and Rehabilitation (CDCR) defines gangs as "any ongoing formal or informal organization, association, or group of three or more persons, which has a common name or identifying sign or symbol whose members and/or associates, individually or collectively, engage or have engaged, on behalf of that organization, association, or group, in two or more acts, which include planning, organizing, threatening, financing, soliciting, or committing unlawful acts...." (CCR Title 15, SS3000).

They further define prison gangs as "any gang, which originated and has its roots within the department or any other prison system" (CCR Title 15, SS3000).

Let's talk about gangs

Let's face it . . . gangs have been around forever. I would imagine that ever since the dawn of civilization men have come together in groups in an effort to accomplish or overcome. It is the principle of synergy (two can accomplish more than the sum of one times two) and man has used it throughout his history.

Youth gang involvement is not a new phenomenon in the United States. Gangs have been known to exist in our country since the 18th-century. Philadelphia was trying to devise a way to deal with roaming youth disrupting the city in 1791. According to the National School Safety Center, officials in New York City acknowledged having gang problems as early as 1825. The gang problem is not likely to go away soon or to be eliminated easily.

But never before the present time have so many gangs emerged in such sheer numbers and diverse factions and with such high levels of violence and criminality. Criminal gangs are present in all levels of society. It's the way of the world. They range from the small, young, and informal gangs of local neighborhoods, with very little structure and sophistication, to the much larger criminally intent and highly structured gangs of inner cities, and even worse the very militant structured and violent prison gangs that abound in the prison systems and influence street gangs throughout the country. The top end of this underworld society is the criminal cartels such as the Italian Mafia, The Westies, Jamaican Posses, and others. These are huge multi-national underworld organizations with vast amounts of cash and capabilities.

History of the Italian Mafia

The Italian Mafia goes way back to the twelfth century when the first recorded acts of organized crime were reported as occurring. The "Sicilian Vespers" revolution against the French was the beginning of the Sicilian Mafia. Although they were not known by than title "mafia"

2

as of yet, they were well organized and vicious. The mafia concept did not initially include central organization. Instead they were several small groups that governed themselves. They were more of a loose knit society.

The Mafia exercised influence over an area by employing scare tactics. They used many different terrorist methods to bully the people into voting them to public office, where they could utilize the influence of that office for the benefit of their group. As they grew, their access to many positions of influence grew as well as their ability to purchase weapons, influence laws, and bribe officials. Made up of a network of thugs the mafia dominated the Sicilian society by the early nineteenth century.

They developed a strict code of conduct which forbade them from having or attempting any sort of contact or cooperation with the police. This conduct was enforced under the threat of death. They were sworn to secrecy at the time of admission into the group. As they transformed themselves throughout the years, they began to be known as "La Cosa Nostra" (our thing). They became so powerful that Italian authorities' attempts to put a stop to or curtail their activities have been futile. This was mainly due to political corruption and the assassination of judges.

Many of those who escaped attempted prosecutions fled to the United States and established the American Mafia. Notable figures like Joseph Bonanno and Lucky Luciano emerged as the top underworld figures of the American Mafia's early power struggles.

Street gangs

Street gangs in the United States have had a long and complicated history dating back to the 1800s. Today, the most publicized street gangs in America are African-American and Hispanic, but I believe that is because of the rap industry and how they push the thug life in their music and dress. However, the reality is that gangs cross all racial, socio-economic, and geographic boundaries. And another reality is that Latinos make up the greater part of gangs in the United States and are often the most militaristic, violent, and highly structured. It is clear by compiled and convincing evidence that most gangs prey on rivals within the same racial backgrounds . . . black on black, brown on brown, etc.

The first street gangs in the United States began around the early 1800s in New York City, and Chicago had gangs as early as the 1920s. These early gangs were known for their criminal activities, which consisted mostly of thievery and property crimes as drugs were not yet illegal and had no black market value. Once drugs were made illegal by laws such as the 1912 International Opium Convention and the 1919 Volstead Act, gangs began to earn money through the trafficking of these substances. Gang involvement in drug trafficking increased during the 1970s and 1980s, and very few gangs have minimal involvement in the trade.

A wide variety of gangs has existed for centuries here in America as well as abroad. Many poor orphans in Victorian London survived their environment by grouping together in gangs and doing what was necessary to survive. They were the outcast of English society and left to fend for their selves. These kids felt secure in numbers and survived by depending on one another for mutual support and protection. They stole food and picked pockets as a way of survival. Most did not have criminal intentions. Their only goal was to survive in the harsh environment that was thrust upon them.

At the end of the day all gangs pretty much have the same goals, intents and purposes, and hunger for power and money. The only difference is that the bigger they are the bigger their appetites are. They are motivated by racial hatred, greed, and criminality, and they achieve their goals through intimidation, acts of unspeakable violence, and drug activity. They rule with an iron fist within their ranks, because it is not uncommon for those in power to be overthrown by their power hungry underlings. It's a dog eat dog world and they play it well.

Realistically, no one grows up planning to become a gang member, criminal, or murderer. It isn't on a child's to do list, nor does it exist anywhere within the realm of a child's imagination. But the sad fact is that it happens, and it happens quite a lot. The pull of the gangster lifestyle is becoming an all too powerful influence with our youth and contributes to their delinquency in high numbers. They pick it up from their older siblings or the older guys in the neighborhood by watching them act all "thugged" out and getting a sense of false respect for their actions. Those guys in turn are influenced by the more experienced guys coming in and out of prison and having association with the prison gangs. It's an on-going cycle that needs to be stopped dead in its tracks.

National Gang Intelligence Center

Gang Definitions

Street gangs are criminal organizations formed on the street operating throughout the United States.

Prison gangs are criminal organizations that originated within the penal system and operate within correctional facilities throughout the United States, although released members may be operating on the street. Prison gangs are also self-perpetuating criminal entities that can continue their criminal operations outside the confines of the penal system.

Outlaw Motorcycle (OMGs) are organizations whose members use their motorcycle clubs as conduits for criminal enterprises. Although some law enforcement agencies regard only One Percenters as OMGs, the NGIC, for the purpose of this assessment, covers all OMG criminal organizations, including OMG support and puppet clubs.

One Percenter the ATF defines *One Percenters* as any group of motorcyclists who have voluntarily made a commitment to band together to abide by their organization's rules enforced by violence and who engage in activities that bring them and their club into repeated and serious conflict with society and the law. The group must be an ongoing organization, association of three (3) or more persons which have a common interest and/or activity characterized by the commission of or involvement in a pattern of criminal or delinquent conduct. AT F estimates there are approximately 300 One Percenter OMGs in the United States.

Neighborhood/Local Neighborhood or Local street gangs are confined to specific neighborhoods and jurisdictions and often imitate larger, more powerful national gangs. The primary purpose for many neighborhood gangs is drug distribution and sales.

CHAPTER TWO

The impact of gangs

Gangs continue to commit criminal activity, recruit new members in urban, suburban, and rural regions across the United States, and develop criminal associations that expand their influence over criminal enterprises, particularly street-level drug sales. The most notable trends for 2011 have been the overall increase in gang membership, and the expansion of criminal street gangs' control of street-level drug sales and collaboration with rival gangs and other criminal organizations. Gangs are expanding, evolving and posing an increasing threat to US communities nationwide. Many gangs are sophisticated criminal networks with members who are violent, distribute wholesale quantities of drugs, and develop and maintain close working relationships with members and associates of transnational criminal/drug trafficking organizations. Gangs are becoming more violent while engaging in less typical and lower-risk crime, such as prostitution and white-collar crime. Gangs are more adaptable, organized, sophisticated, and opportunistic, exploiting new and advanced technology as a means to recruit, communicate discretely, target their rivals, and perpetuate their criminal activity. Based on state, local, and federal law enforcement reporting, the NGIC concludes that:

- There are approximately 1.4 million active street, prison, and OMG gang members comprising more than 33,000 gangs in the United States. Gang membership increased most significantly in the Northeast and Southeast regions, although the West and Great Lakes regions boast the highest number of gang members. Neighborhood- based gangs, hybrid gang

7

members, and national-level gangs such as the Sureños are rapidly expanding in many jurisdictions. Many communities are also experiencing an increase in ethnic-based gangs such as African, Asian, Caribbean, and Eurasian gangs.

- Gangs are responsible for an average of 48 percent of violent crime in most jurisdictions and up to 90 percent in several others, according to NGIC analysis. Major cities and suburban areas experience the most gang-related violence. Local neighborhood-based gangs and drug crews continue to pose the most significant criminal threat in most communities. Aggressive recruitment of juveniles and immigrants, alliances and conflict between gangs, the release of incarcerated gang members from prison, advancements in technology and communication, and Mexican Drug Trafficking Organization (MDTO) involvement in drug distribution have resulted in gang expansion and violence in a number of jurisdictions.

- Gangs are increasingly engaging in non-traditional gang-related crime, such as alien smuggling, human trafficking, and prostitution. Gangs are also engaging in white collar crime such as counterfeiting, identity theft, and mortgage fraud, primarily due to the high profitability and much lower visibility and risk of detection and punishment than drug and weapons trafficking.

- US-based gangs have established strong working relationships with Central American and MDTOs to perpetrate illicit cross-border activity, as well as with some organized crime groups in some regions of the United States. US-based gangs and MDTOs are establishing wide-reaching drug networks; assisting in the smuggling of drugs, weapons, and illegal immigrants along the Southwest Border; and serving as enforcers for MDTO interests on the US side of the border.

- Many gang members continue to engage in gang activity while incarcerated. Family members play pivotal roles in assisting or facilitating gang activities and recruitment during a gang members' incarceration. Gang members in some correctional facilities are adopting radical religious views while incarcerated.

- Gangs encourage members, associates, andrelatives to obtain law enforcement, judiciary, or legal employment in order to gather information on rival gangs and law enforcement operations. Gang infiltration of the military continues to pose a significant criminal threat, as members of at least 53 gangs have been identified on both domestic and international military installations. Gang members who learn advanced weaponry and combat techniques in the military are at risk of employing these skills on the street when they return to their communities.
- Gang members are acquiring high-powered, military-style weapons and equipment which poses a significant threat because of the potential to engage in lethal encounters with law enforcement officers and civilians. Typically firearms are acquired through illegal purchases; straw purchases via surrogates or middle-men, and thefts from individuals, vehicles, residences and commercial establishments. Gang members also target military and law enforcement officials, facilities, and vehicles to obtain weapons, ammunition, body armor, police gear, badges, uniforms, and official identification.
- Gangs on Indian Reservations often emulate national-level gangs and adopt names and identifiers from nationally recognized urban gangs. Gang members on some Indian Reservations are associating with gang members in the community to commit crime.
- Gangs are becoming increasingly adaptable and sophisticated, employing new and advanced technology to facilitate criminal activity discreetly, enhance their criminal operations, and connect with other gang members, criminal organizations, and potential recruits nationwide and even worldwide.

Effects of Gangs

Paul Bright has been freelance writing online since 2006, specializing in topics related to military employment, mental health and gardens. He writes for various websites. He is also a federal employee in Northern California. Bright holds a Bachelor of Science in psychology from the University of North Carolina-Pembroke and is pursuing a Master of Arts in psychology-marriage and family therapy from Brandman University.

By Paul Bright, eHow Contributor

Gangs can have a tremendous effect on society. They have existed for hundreds of years, especially in America. Although gangs are usually created from people who intend to offer safety in numbers, this safety is usually done through acts of crime. This article will explain how gangs and their activities affect society.

History
- *Gangs have been in existence since the dawn of man. It has never been unusual to see small bands of men protect each other through committing crimes that sometimes involve violence. Gangs in the United States have existed since the 1800s. In the Western regions, gangs of people used to rob trains of passenger's money. They would also steal cattle from unsuspecting cowboys. Other cultural gangs formed on the East Coast as immigrants poured into large, urban cities. The movie "Gangs of New York" was a historically based film that outlined those gangs. The Capone gang and other mobsters began terrorizing neighborhoods in the early 1900s. Today, many American gangs are formed not only in cities but in suburban neighborhoods as well with the common purpose of dealing drugs.*

Function
- *A gang usually functions through high levels of organization and within their specific cultures. The Mafia, for example, was mostly limited to Catholic Italians from Sicily. The*

New York gangs of the mid-1800s were drawn from their immigrant and non-immigrant statuses such as Irishmen and those who considered themselves "natives" of America. Organization is typically made up of one head per "family" that evenly divides territory among other gangs within the culture. The head usually has one other member seen as the number-two man. Underneath those two are several captains that are in charge of any moneymaking operations that the head man authorizes to take place.

Effects

o *Gangs of all levels and types usually have a negative effect on society. Gangs, gang violence and gang wars typically suck up a city or town's police resources because of the sheer number of people involved, lack of witness cooperation and types of crimes connected to gangs. Higher-level gangs that are investigated by the FBI sometimes force the agency to utilize very risky and very expensive resources like high-tech surveillance, informants and witness protection programs.*

Gangs also can bring down the property value of neighborhoods from the violence and vandalism involved with gang life. Big money investors may shy away from places where they feel that their properties and resources will not be used for fear of gang crimes. Gangs can also drive up prices of local groceries and commodities via their intimidating schemes that force businesses to pay them sums of money in exchange for "protection."

Prevention/Solution

o *Teenage gang prevention often involves early intervention by special at-risk programs that offer mentorship and activities to do after school. If teens feel that they can find summer jobs and fun activities that will keep them off of the streets, they may choose to participate rather than join a gang that could get them arrested or killed.*

For older gangs that are more organized or commit more violent crimes, prevention usually involves getting the community to protect itself. Communities need to be willing to inform police of suspicious activities and not create environments where gangs can thrive, such as towns with low wages or little aesthetic pride. If people feel that they have equal opportunities to succeed and educate themselves, gangs are less likely to exist.

Warning
    o   *Gangs can become violent quickly. They can use violence as a technique of intimidation for not just one person but all people in the neighborhood or town. Do not attempt to be a hero and take a gang down single-handed. Organizing neighborhood watches and keeping in contact with police can deter a gang from causing trouble. If more and more gang members lose their numbers to the penitentiary and have fewer people to recruit, they are likely to dissolve*

Read more: Effects of Gangs | eHow.com http://www.ehow.com

Are you willing to be the one who loses? The one who gets burned? The one who takes the fall? Is acceptance that important? Sure you just might possibly ball for a minute . . . floss and high side . . . but the chances for success and survival really suck and once you are down, there is no revival . . . only collateral damage and existence within the depths of inhumanity . . . the land of the lost . . . straight stuck! Sitting in the penitentiary or in a body bag. Living in a concrete jungle in an atmosphere of extreme violence and anger. These are the real costs of being a thug and gang member. Is temporary gratification worth all of this? Really? Think about it. Take heed!

And what about your families? Do they have that coming? Should they have to bear the brunt of your mistakes? No . . . I don't think so! We should cherish our families for who they are and what they are to us. Fathers/mentors, mothers/nurturers, sisters and brothers/loving peers, wives/bff's (best friends forever), and children/treasures . . . our loved ones. Do not repay their love with sorrow, pain, and heartache. Share your life with them . . . don't rob them of it. Sometimes we don't appreciate what we have until it is taken away from us. I know that it took me a lifetime to realize that my wife, my son, and my girls are a treasure to me and now I have my grandchildren to cherish.

But I am here to tell you that you will regret not appreciating them once you step into the shoes I have worn. Because of the many years that I lived as a thug and gang member, I lost over fifty percent of my mother's life. My father was such a stranger to me that I could not even address him as father, but rather called him by his first name. My siblings (I have four) grew up in my absence. They went from the little boys and girls that I knew in my childhood to the grown adults and pretty much strangers that I know today. I have nieces and nephews who are adults whom I have just recently met for the very first time. All pretty much are strangers. I lost the treasure of their childhoods and when I look over photos of their passing years my heart gets filled with regret.

My daughters and son are grown adults with families of their own. I am fortunate to have changed my ways now while my grandchildren are young, so that I may at least experience the treasure of their lives. My behaviors have taken their toll on my wife, whom I love very much. The stress of my life has affected her physical health and well-being. I am fortunate to have her still here and I will cherish that always.

But the sad thing is that I also victimized my brothers and sisters by taking away their older brother and turning him into a complete stranger. There is an uneasiness that permeates the air when we get to together, and I'm sure that time will heal that wound, but the fact is that it is there, and I put it there by my behaviors over the years. It really breaks my heart, but I must live with it and deal with it on my own terms. I have no one else to blame but myself for the mistakes I have made in my life. They are all living their lives and raising their children and even though I know that they love me, it seems as if I don't fit, because I took me away from them and they grew and lived with a part time son, brother, uncle, husband, father, and grandfather.

Yes the loss of family and the loss of one's freedom is a disheartening combination. Some can deal with it as a matter of survival, even though it hurts and crushes the spirit. Others go off the deep end. Prisons are filled with those who have to depend on psychotropic medications to get them through the day. Their personal anguish is overwhelming and the, grappling hook of their medications, keep them buoyant, yet on the very brink of drowning in self-pity. For some even that is not enough. They find themselves at the short end of a braided sheet or the sharpened end of a razor blade, taking their own lives to stop the misery they wallow in. Don't be fooled . . . it happens quite a lot in prison, and to people you wouldn't think would ever take that route.

Quite a different story from the care-free flossing thug that first stepped up to the game. Does that sound terrible? It should . . . because it is. But it is also the reality and there is no way around it. We have to face it head on . . . one on one . . . with those at risk. The loss of family is by far the worse punishment that can be inflicted . . . and sadly . . . it is most times self-inflicted. Few are fortunate that their families stick by them through it all. But the loss is still felt, no matter how much contact one has with family, even though the contact in prison is limited to a few hours per week. Others have no contact at all and must fend for themselves in a predatorily hostile environment. No letters from loved ones, no visits, no phone calls, and no financial support. It is harsh . . . think about it.

©©©
Stranger in the house . . .
Just got out of prison.
Looking at my kid's . . .
At what I been missing.
©©©
All of those years . . .
Spent behind the walls.
Not being there . . .
When family calls.
©©©
Little baby's birthdays . . .
Spent without dad.
The years have gone by . . .
Gee that's so sad.
©©©

Stranger in the house . . .
Trying to get caught up.
Don't be like me . . .
Don't drink from this cup.
©©©
It's got a bitter taste . . .
Even hard to swallow.
Loss of family . . .
Pretty hard to follow.
I'm a . . .
Stranger in the house.
©©©

The trick is to realize that you are headed in the wrong direction before you cross that bridge, and believe me; all gangsters will cross that bridge sooner or later. It's inevitable. So get your head together before it's too late. Do the right thing and change your ways now. Don't wait or procrastinate or you'll soon find yourself sitting in the S.H.U., just like I did. Validated . . . caught up in the game . . . in the politics . . . where life pretty much sucks. Don't believe me? You should because I lived it for over two decades.

And now I am a "drop-out". Dropping out at that stage of the game has its ups and downs as well. I have to be aware of my surroundings at all times and who is around me, as I have a "green light" (order to be hit) on me by the very gang that I was a part of for many years. They don't take too kindly to members dropping out of the game. Even out here in the streets, I have to be careful where I go and what I do, so that I do not put myself in harm's way.

Yes Sir! The boys on the block might just seem to be an innocent gathering of friends, but that's where it starts. And it only gets worse from there. Just walk past them; they don't have anything you could possibly want in your life. Just do you and do it in a positive and productive way. They're just hanging out . . . going with the flow . . . and most often, the flow is not something positive or up-building. Flying colors, representing, drinking, and getting loaded or lit, and off they go! Headed for a wreck somewhere. There is no defined road map or set format to becoming a gang member. It just sort of happens . . . if you allow it to happen.

15

Most people evolve into a gang member . . . some don't, but never the less the exposure is there. The fortunate ones are the ones who made a decision early on that they would rise above the neighborhood, the circumstances, and the exposure to become someone special. They made sound decisions based on solid values and principles that they learned from their parents or in school. The continued forward in their lives despite the roadblocks. Unfortunately, they are the exception.

We all learn and grow by emulating our parents, our siblings, and our peers. Who are you going to emulate? That is the question. We pick up customs, language, habits, and gestures, both good and bad. All that we see that goes on around us has a profound effect on who we become as people. Racism, hatred, indecency, immorality, and on, and on. We pick things up like a sponge, some intentional, others not so intentional. Without the rudder of parental guidance, we begin to mirror those behaviors that are not conducive to a proper up-bringing. Only proper guidance with Christian principles can combat these negative influences.

Everything in our schools, in our neighborhoods, and in our activities can have a direct bearing in who we become. When attitudes or events are acceptable to others around us, they usually wind up becoming acceptable to us as well, without any proper guidance. So as we are growing up and we see the "homies" on the block, kicking it, drinking, wearing colors, smoking weed, and selling and doing drugs, etc., and no one is doing anything about it (I don't mean the Police, I mean the people who live in that neighborhood), or saying anything about it, we tend to see them as acceptable, and may often do as they do.

With that said I think the obvious first line of defense should be in the neighborhood and in the homes of those neighborhoods. If we can nip it in the bud at home and in our neighborhoods, we have a good chance of stopping the growth of gangs in the future. The system has failed and unless we do something about it, it will continue to fail for many more of our kids. New laws get enacted but still fail to do the job. Prison isn't the answer, although I believe that prisons do serve a purpose. The answer lies within our homes and neighborhoods . . . within ourselves!

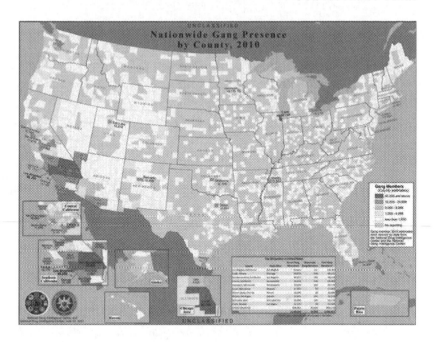

Source: NGIC and NDIC 2010 National Drug Survey Data

Gang Summit hosted by the US Department of Justice

October 23, 2006

On September 24 of this year, Los Angeles experienced a new low.

Three-year old Kaitlyn Avila was shot point-blank by a gang member who mistakenly thought her father was a member of a rival gang.

The gang member shot and wounded her father, then intentionally fired into little Kaitlyn's chest. This is the first time law enforcement officials remember a young child being "targeted" in a gang shooting.

This shooting is but a symptom of the disease that has taken hold of our cities—and that disease is gang violence. The violence perpetrated by gang members on one another, on police officers and on innocent bystanders is horrifying.

Gang violence is an attack not only on individuals, but also on our communities.

It stops mothers from allowing their children to play outside. It prevents the elderly from taking walks in their neighborhoods. It creates an environment of fear.

It is well past time for the federal government to provide a hand of assistance to state and local law enforcement. It is well past time to come to grips with the escalating levels of violence.

The key is a balanced, comprehensive approach.

First, we must help those on the front lines. This means new laws, tougher penalties, and millions for investigations and prosecutions.

Second, we must identity and fund successful community programs. These are programs like the Gang Risk Intervention Program— GRIP—at Lennox Middle School in Inglewood, which I visited in August.

The program's results are clear: 80% of participants graduated high school and stayed away from gangs. Students in the program were truant less often, and also showed improvement in their work habits and grades.

We've got to replicate successful programs like this one across the country.

And third, we must make it safer for witnesses to come forward and testify. You can't win cases, if witnesses fear for their life.

Many of you know that I've been working on gang legislation for several years. Yet, the bill has not become law.

So today, I'd like to talk about the scope of the problem; to let you know what I believe can be done to help stem the tide; and to ask for your help in getting a new, comprehensive law approved.

The latest FBI statistics are in. Violent crime is on the rise— Murders are up. Robberies are up. Aggravated assaults are up.

This is true in every region in the country, and the increases are greater than any year since 1991.

And a big reason for the rise? Gangs have metastasized from the big cities like Los Angeles and Chicago to the medium and small ones. Places like Milwaukee, Birmingham, Cleveland, and St. Louis.

There are now at least 30,000 gangs nationwide, with 800,000 members.

In California, there are 3,700 gangs up and down the State. 171,000 juveniles and adults are committed to this criminal way of life.

That's greater than the population of 28 counties, and the same number of people that live in the City of Tracy.

You are all too aware of the damage that gangs do. From 1992 to 2003, there were more than 7,500 gang-related homicides reported in California. That's equivalent to the entire city of Sausalito.

And in 2004, more than one-third (of the 2,000) homicides in California (698) were gang-related. It's worse among our young. Nearly 50 percent of the murders of 18-29 year olds were gang-related. And nearly 60 percent of the murders of teens under 18 were gang-related.

Now, the rate of gang violence is not always the same everywhere.

There has been a recent drop in gang membership and gang violence in Los Angeles, for example. This is good news, but it is likely just a blip on the radar. Gang roots run deep in Los Angeles, and these gains may only be temporary.

When you look at the big picture, you see that gangs continue to infiltrate our communities.

It is estimated that gangs are now having an impact on at least 2,500 communities across the nation.

They control neighborhoods through violence. They traffic in drugs, theft, extortion, prostitution, guns, and murder.

All too often this puts law enforcement in danger. Let me name but a few:

- *Los Angeles Police Officer Ricardo Lizarraga. Killed while responding to a domestic violence call, by a man who drew a gun and shot him twice in the back. The suspect was a known member of the Rollin20s Bloods.*
- *Merced Police Officer Stephan Gray. Officer Gray was shot and killed when a suspect (a gang member he had encountered before) fired two bullets into his chest.*

The list goes on:

- *Los Angeles Sherriff's Deputy Jeffrey Ortiz.*
- *Burbank Police Officer Matthew Pavelka.*
- *California Highway Patrol Officer Thomas Steiner.*
- *And San Francisco Police Officer Isaac Espinoza.*
  Los Angeles Police Department Chief Bill Bratton put it bluntly: "There is nothing more insidious than these gangs. They are worse than the Mafia. Show me a year in New York where the Mafia indiscriminately killed 300 people. You can't."

The problem is immense. It is on the streets. It is in the prisons. It is in big cities and small. It is in California, and every other State.

So we've got to come up with a comprehensive approach.

Here are the key questions:

How do we keep our youth out of these gangs in the first place?

How do we encourage and protect witnesses who come forward and testify?

And what do we do when the gangs perpetrate violence in our communities?
It is clear to me that a commitment has to be made on each of these fronts.
We know that a coordinated approach like this works. You have no further to look than Modesto for results:

In Modesto, community leaders put in place a model built on suppression, intervention and prevention. They established a law enforcement task force. They brought together police, sheriff, the DA, parole, and corrections. They were able to create a database on gang members and use that shared intelligence to coordinate enforcement efforts.

They established a community task force to make sure every elementary school had an after-school prevention program. They put sheriff's deputies into the middle and high schools, creating a constant visual presence.
This balanced approach has worked. Murders have dropped from 24 in 2003 and Drive-by shootings have fallen 88%. Gang-related gun assaults have dropped by two-thirds from their peak.

The gang bill I am sponsoring would encourage this kind of balanced approach.
Senator Orrin Hatch of Utah and I first introduced legislation in 1996. And I have introduced a gang bill in each Congress since that time.

Along the way, we have gotten close. Many of the provisions of our gang bill were incorporated into the 1999 Juvenile Justice bill, which was approved overwhelmingly (73-25) by the Senate in the 106th Congress.
But the bill stalled in Conference, and these provisions were never signed into law.

In 2004, our bill was approved by the Senate Judiciary Committee, but once again it stalled. And in this Congress, we worked with members of both sides of the aisle to develop a bill that enjoys broader support than we have had in the past. And we will reintroduce this legislation in the early days of the next Congress. So what would this bill do?

Simply put, it would be a balanced program—with new programs and funding for prosecutions, and support for programs to prevent people from joining gangs in the first place.
2004 to only six in 2005 and 2006

The Department of Justice announced this Spring that it was devoting $30 million in new funds to fight gangs, including $2.5 million in Los Angles.

This is welcome, but it is but a drop in the bucket. So the bill I have introduced would authorize almost 30 times the DOJ's initiative—$870 million for all activities over five years. $500 million of that would be used to create new "High Intensity Interstate Gang Activity Areas."

These would mirror the successful HIDTA (High Intensity Drug Trafficking Area) model that brings together federal, state and local agents to coordinate investigations and prosecutions. And the $500 million would be split 50/50, so that for every dollar spent on law enforcement, a dollar would be spent on prevention.

Simply put, we would try to replicate and expand the state and local models that have worked in the past.
And we would establish a clearinghouse to collect "best practices," so that this isn't theory, but what works on the street.

The bill would also authorize $100 million for Project Safe Neighborhoods, a Justice Department program designed to reduce gun violence in America. But at the same time, this bill would establish new crimes and tougher federal penalties.

Today's federal street gang laws are weak, and are almost never used. Currently, a person committing a gang crime might have extra time tacked on to the end of their federal sentence. This is because federal law currently focuses on gang violence as a sentencing enhancement, rather than a crime unto itself.
So the bill I have offered would make it a separate federal crime for any criminal street gang member to commit, conspire or attempt to commit violent crimes—including murder, kidnapping, arson, extortion—in furtherance of the gang.
And the penalties for gang members committing such crimes would increase considerably.

- *For gang-related murder, the penalty would be life imprisonment or the death penalty.*
- *For kidnapping, aggravated sexual abuse or maiming, or if death resulted, the penalties would be from 5 years to life imprisonment.*
- *For any other serious violent felony, the penalty would be 3-30 years.*
- *And for any crime of violence—defined as the actual or intended use of physical force against the person of another—the penalty would run from 0-20 years. The bill would also:*

- *Create a new crime for recruiting juveniles and adults into a criminal street gang. Currently, there is no federal crime that covers this.*
- *This bill would change that, by making recruiting gang members a new federal crime, with a penalty of 0-10 years. If someone recruited a minor, the penalty would be 1-20 years. And if someone recruited from prison, the penalty would be 5-20 years, and would be consecutive to their existing sentence.*

  The bill would create new federal crimes for:
  - *committing multiple interstate murders;*
  - *crossing state lines to obstruct justice; and*
  - *committing violent crimes in connection with drug trafficking (whether or not it is gang-related).*

- *The bill would also increase the penalties for "RICO" (Racketeering Influenced and Corrupt Organizations)-related crimes, so that they match the new penalties the bill establishes for gang crimes.*
  This balanced approach—of prevention plus tough penalties—will send a clear message to gang members.

Hardened gang members can take advantage of the opportunities we are creating, with schools and social services agencies empowered to make alternatives to gangs a realistic option.

But if they continue to engage in violence, they will face serious consequences.
The bill would also provide $270 million in funds for witness protection grants.

Too often, witnesses are afraid to come forward and tell the truth due to fear.
State and local law enforcement officers lack the resources needed to protect the safety of such witnesses and informants.

> *So this legislation will be a clear-eyed approach to tackle all aspects of the problem.*
>
> *Bottom line: the growth in size and complexity of gangs has become a national problem, requiring a federal response.*
> *http://feinstein.senate.gov/06speeches/s-gang-violence1023.htm*

Family values are not what they used to be. But who is to blame? Our economic woes? Our parents lack of commitment to family cohesiveness? Our much too permissive society? Can it really be pin-pointed to an exact cause? I doubt it. It is the agglomeration of all of these issues and even more that weave an intricate pattern of disruption of the family values that existed just a half century ago. Those values have been consistently eroded year after year in the name of social change and improvement. I definitely see the change, but the improvement is very questionable. Just look around you and you'll see what I'm talking about. Sexual immorality is at an all-time high.

Thievery is common place among business professionals, and the list goes on and on. We must as a society and as parents, see the writing on the wall and do what we must to stop the insanity and reverse the trend. It has gotten so bad that children no longer respect their parents or authority of any kind.

Gang Violence

Gang violence is a problem in every major city in the United States and membership is on the rise. According to the Department of Justice's 2005 National Gang Threat Assessment, there are at least 21,500 gangs and more than 731,000 active gang members. While gangs are less prevalent in rural areas, in major cities, gang violence is responsible for roughly half of all homicides. Gangs are also becoming more savvy, using computers and other technology to commit crimes.

Gathering accurate statistics on gangs and gang membership is difficult for a number of reasons. Gangs obviously don't keep official records of their membership. Some people hang out with gang members, but aren't actually in a gang themselves. If someone "runs with" a gang, but hasn't been initiated yet, is that person a member? Who do you count when compiling your statistics?

It's also important to consider the source of the data. If a police officer asks a gang member, "Are you in a gang?" chances are the gang member will say no, knowing that police place extra scrutiny on known gang members. Some youths may claim gang membership around other teens to seem tough, and gangs might inflate membership numbers to make their gang seem more powerful. Police departments don't always report gang statistics accurately, either. Federal grants for fighting gang violence can give departments incentive to exaggerate gang numbers, while some departments deny having any gang problems at all to appease the public.

The pictures below are a "before and after" shot to show that even if you can clean up an area, it is difficult to "KEEP" it clean. Is it possible to build the capacity of a family to move away from 'their mind set' and change? How does a long-term answer emerge, and what can we learn from these sets of pictures? GXG Teams worked with this crew as they slowly changed. Eventually they were unable to 'hold' their territory, and were publicly were jacked (1998). Now, 8 years later, they are back.

WE had some crews who made it ... and so, why not this one?

The picture on the right is from the same place on the left. This site was cleaned up in 1998 but by 2006 it was back to it's old state.

---

*In 1997 we learned that, with love, you can effectively influence a person Gang affiliated. Originally, we did intervention, and then learned prevention was even **more** important. If we didn't target their little brothers and sisters, it was only a matter of time, till the incarcerated uncles, and cousins, come home. Kids are affected by their role models (Those who are available, influence them).*

*To change a neighborhood, we need more then basic Juvenile Services: We need a weed **and the 'seed'**. We found we couldn't do it all ourselves and we needed others to sustain a long term change. If we had linked to other services quicker, we could have responded to more families. Generational gangsters, can be changed with love. **An ounce of prevention, is better then a pound of intervention.***

How Does This Relate To Why Kids Join Gangs?

Gangs are only a byproduct of individual sharing the same beliefs, or at least having commonalities. We could take a gang of 10-20 members and sit them down separately for questioning and ask them each: "Why did you join a gang?", and would probably get 2-3 common answers.

The need for Family (Belonging)
The need for Protection (Security)
The need for Popularity (Mass Acceptance)

There are other sub-reasons such as Peer Pressure, Vengeance, Self-Destruction (Loss of Concern), AND Generational Involvement.

Now, a child does not sit down and compare gangs within his/her area to decide which one to join. It doesn't work that way. So how do they bridge to a crew? The process typically looks like this:

1. Living life with needs unmet, conclusions, belief systems.
2. Make Friends (6 yrs - 13 yrs.)
3. Finds a group to relate & connect with
4. Attaches his/herself with group (gangs for some)

Living Conditions + responses, = our present life. What are the visible options?

It is less than admirable, what our world has quickly become in regards to molding the minds of our youth. Sometimes we want wring the necks of the TV people who make heroes out of smart-alecky kids, who treat their parents like idiots. The TV is a class room that gives our children pointers on how to out- think and to manipulate others. The community at large is inheriting youth who are practicing how they can 'take' center stage, to get the attention they deserve . . . at any price.

Some youth, need a Motivational Rewrite that can help them identify rewarding goals, by having peers present realistic options? After we initially link through any of the partnerships, we need to help plug them into available follow-up clinics and workshops that will empower youth to continue building their capacity to succeed for the challenges ahead.

Together we can help Youth Identify Means & Steps towards Accomplishing These Goals. What VGPP has made available, is visible youth trainers, who can help our At-Risk youth make better decisions and demonstrate how to live more productive and safer lives. Together, our combined services can teach Youth Coping Skills that help build a balanced response.

For some, joining a gang somehow temporarily satisfies the needs listed above. Between the adolescent and teenage years, resources are few, so Neighborhood Networks become one of the few resources that they can reach easily and pull from to "fix" the problem (unmet needs).

Many choose to not see or ignore help.

VGPP have developed workshops that serve small groups or individuals to help get and keep them out of a gang. Building a support group network is a key to Community or personal survival.

A Community Network really mobilizes our neighborhoods' ability to help reduce violent behaviors and lifestyles; after school & in the streets. On way to or from school, latch-key and no-key kids will benefit from this enhanced violence free areas.

It's Time to Respond!

TODAY, we have the opportunity to change this equation by getting involved. We can slow down the assembly line of the family downward spiral. We can do this together!

WE NEED to do this, TODAY. If we are going to continue to rediscover the problem, without addressing it, then we are on our own treadmill. A rut is a grave without the ends put in, (yet). The final word hasn't been written on this, IF you will respond. Our youth have an option, if we make it AVAILABLE AND VISIBLE.

Let's focus on what is working and find our place as part of the regional solution. Whatever each team specializes in, regardless of their capacity to serve, everyone is a resource. All are valuable.

- What do you have to offer as a resource, and where do you fit in?
- Are you capable of training other teams to build their capacity, or do you need to have your teams receive further training?
- Is it possible that we provide that for each other? Can you go to our web site, and Plug in? If you want to volunteer, or to raise funding, or to have a trainer come, we are ready.
- Can you train others? Why not partner for a more complete response to those who would contact any of us? We need to identify those coordinators, who are committed to help other's build their capacity, and then help them get trained - to train others.
- Where are you in this process, and can we help you? http://godsxgangsters.org/gangs/InformationAboutGangs.htm

©©©
Evil ways creeping . . .
Doing drugs and dealing.
Hangin' and bangin' . . .
Robbing and stealing.
©©©
The ways of our youth . . .
The games that they play.
They haven't a clue . . .
And that's how they'll stay.
©©©
So it's all up to us . . .
To get their lives straight.
To teach them to love . . .
Not to fight and to hate.
©©©
To teach them the values . . .
Of life as we know.
To give them direction . . .
And fill them with hope.
©©©
For they are our future . . .
Need I say more?

CHAPTER THREE

The gang culture

So now that we know what gangs are in the literal sense of the word, let's go even further and examine gangs and the gang culture from the perspective and several decades of personal experience of a **former gang member** (myself) as well as other research avenues that are available. However, first I would like my readers to understand that this is not some self-glorification trip that I am on. I truly regret my life as a gang-member and the crimes I committed in association with that. That being said, if I can turn the life of just one child away from the gravitational pull of gangs or convince one person to push forward and strive to guide a lost child, my life would have been worth it.

This book is merely an attempt to reach the truth about gangs, gang involvement, and its far-reaching influence in hopes of exposing it to those who need to be enlightened, It is an attempt to provide **guidance, intervention,** and **prevention** for those who are living, or about to step into this reality. I lived the life, and I know its deadly consequences from the ramifications of early childhood gang involvement to the much later deadly environment of prison gang involvement. I don't want one more child to step into the shoes that I stepped into, so as a matter of conscience, I must write this book.

Included in this book are several poems which I have written regarding gang involvement and prevention as well as enlightenment. They are my personal writings and are placed in here as a message to our youth.

Criminal minds . . .
Leaving behind,
Death and destruction . . .
Their only function,
©©©
To hurt and to harm . . .
Raise an alarm?
It really should . . .
For it's understood,
©©©
That bad brings worse.
It's a criminal curse . . .
The life that he lives.
No one forgives . . .
©©©
Not even him . . .
He knows it's a sin.
Just doesn't care . . .
Spreads hate everywhere.

Right now he doesn't . . .
Not till he deposits . . .
His life in a cage.
Where convicts engage . . .
©©©
In hatred and murder.
Let's carry it further . . .
A little past that.
He never comes back . . .
©©©
Placed in a casket . . .
Cause he got blasted.
By another young fool . . .
Whose mind was so cruel.
©©©
Is this what you choose?
The criminal blues?

Gangs have taken America by storm and run rampant among all ethnicities, in all cities, and among all socio-economic levels. Gangs are, by their very definition, undesirable, repugnant, intimidating, and oppressive. They prey on innocent people who work hard for what they have. They rob society of peace of mind and personal security. They kill one another indiscriminately, without any concern for the collateral damage they cause. They run unchecked through our neighborhoods engaged in criminal activity. Yet, they continue to thrive and multiply in our neighborhoods in the face of massive law enforcement efforts to curb the trend. It is a huge rising storm that threatens to engulf and inundate our society . . . or maybe . . . they already have.

We must not let ourselves entertain these thoughts until they come to fruition. That is why the gang culture is so prevalent and influencing. Our youths are bombarded with negative thoughts on a continuing basis, and they eventually act out on those thoughts. We need to help our youth to break away from the embrace of gangs and the negative thoughts that emanate from that culture. And in order to accomplish this, we must head back to the morality of yesteryear.

As previously stated, there were gangs back then as well, but their presence was not so well accepted and exploited. Yes . . . I said exploited. They are exploited for the sake of making money because it is what sells on television, rap music, movies, video games, and books. There are even web sites dedicated solely to individual gangs. Just type gangs in your Internet search box and see what pops up. You'll be astounded. Do you think your kids do not go there? Get real . . . they all go there . . . even if just out of curiosity. There are so many avenues of exposure to the gang culture that one cannot even begin to count them. Gangs even recruit on social-networking sites.

I have two daughters and in their formative teenage years, I fought with them tooth and nail because they both were gravitating to the Norteno culture. Who can blame them? I was a prime example for them to emulate. I would find Norteno gang CD's such as Seventeen Reasons or G.U.N. (Generation of United Nortenos) in their things, or I would catch little signs such as wearing red shoe laces and red scrungees in their hair. They were associating with teens identified as gang members in their schools. However, because I was up on all of that, and I fought hard with them, I was able to save them from my insanity. They are both now responsible adults with post-high school degrees and achievements and are doing well in their careers in the medical field.

I was savvy to all the hype and it was still a tough battle for me to win, so can you imagine how much harder it is for a person who isn't up on the game to recognize the signs of eminent gang involvement? It's not an easy thing to see. The culture is so prevalent that to the unseeing eye it seems like normal activity. How are parents who are naïve supposed to recognize the signs? That is what this book is about. Parents need to be given the appropriate tools in order to successfully protect their children for the influence of gangs.

Why Do People Join Gangs?

There are many possible reasons for someone to join a gang, but four primary reasons seem to describe most gang members: Many gangs exist mainly as a moneymaking enterprise. By committing thefts and dealing drugs, gang members can make relatively large amounts of money in a very short time. People who are faced with a lack of money may turn to crime if they can't earn enough with a legitimate job. This partly explains why gangs exist in poor, rundown areas of cities. However, not everyone who is poor joins a gang, and not every gang member is poor. Other reasons why our youth become gang members include: lack of positive role models; low self-esteem; physical safety/security; peer relations; sense of identity; increased status; opportunities for excitement; and making fast money, especially by selling drugs. The explosion of youth gangs and gang-related crime has had a tremendous impact on juvenile correctional facilities. Juvenile justice officials are confronted with increasing numbers of gang-involved youths being committed to their facilities. They are becoming more dangerous at an early age and have no respect for authority.

Gang members tend to be young. This is partly because gangs intentionally recruit teenagers, but it's also because young people are very susceptible to peer pressure. If they live in a gang-dominated area, or go to a school with a strong gang presence, they might find that many of their friends are joining gangs. It can be difficult for a teen to understand the harm that joining a gang can bring if he's worried about losing all of his friends. Many teenagers do resist the temptation of gang membership, but for others it is easier to follow the crowd. Peer pressure is a driving force behind gang membership in affluent areas.

With nothing else to occupy their time, youths sometimes turn to mischief to entertain themselves. If gangs are already present in the neighborhood, that can provide an outlet. Alternatively, teenagers might form their own gangs. This is why many communities have tried to combat gangs by simply giving kids something to do. Dances, sports tournaments and other youth outreach programs can literally keep kids off the streets. Unfortunately, many youths and even gang experts use boredom as an excuse. Authors of articles about gang violence often write something like, "There's nothing else to do where they live." Indeed, youth sports programs, swimming pools or even libraries are often in short supply or poor repair in tough urban areas. But for every teenager who gets bored and joins a gang, there are 10 who find positive, productive ways to spend their time.

If poverty is a condition, despair is a state of mind. People who have always lived in poverty with parents who lived in poverty often see no chance of ever getting a decent job, leaving their poor neighborhood or getting an education. They are surrounded by drugs and gangs, and their parents may be addicts or non-responsive. A neighborhood gang can seem like the only real family they'll ever have. Joining a gang gives them a sense of belonging and being a part of something important that they can't get otherwise. In some cases, parents approve of their children joining gangs, and may have been a member of the same gang in the past.

There are many reasons besides those stated above why people join gangs. There are environmental and socio-economic factors, parental and societal values, or lack there-of, and individual morals and attitudes that come into play to contribute to the undue delinquency of our youth. It is my personal belief however, that the number one factor contributing to the high number of young men and women getting involved with gangs is the social permissiveness of today's world.

As a society we have become too permissive on our attitudes, morals, and values. This in turn sets the scenario that is conducive to the growth and spread of gangs, gang behavior, and the gang culture. Our youth see society's non-action toward gang behavior (i.e. thug mentality, gangster rap, stacking chips, etc.) as a stamp of approval for them to go after those things. Gangster Rap glorifies murder, drug dealing, thuggish behavior, and belittles women and the youth of today pick up on that very quickly. Since no one is stepping up to the plate and telling them that this is the wrong type of attitude to have, most of them just go with it.

Incorrigible youth . . .
Way out of line.
Our battle to lose . . .
If we don't define,
©©©
A well thought out plan . . .
To bring them all back,
From where they ran . . .
Because of our slack.
©©©
In the company of . . .
Gangs, drugs, and violence.
Enough is enough!
Let's not be silent.
©©©
Not anymore . . .
It'll only get worse.
That's what's in store . . .
If we don't disperse,
©©©
The gangs and the clicques,
That have formed . . .
From all of our kids.
A huge rising storm.
©©©
That engulfs us, you see.
Unless we stand up . . .
And fight readily.
It surely won't stop.
©©©
All of us lose . . .
So there's no excuse!

CHAPTER FOUR

Types and Structure of Gangs

Many street gangs consist of people with similar backgrounds, race, and motivations. Some grow up as friends from early childhood and as a group, begin to gravitate toward the gang culture. The term street gang is commonly interchanged with youth gang, referring to neighborhood or street-based youth groups that meet the "gang" criteria. However, do not be fooled for behind each one of those youthful gang members is a "Veterano" (older more sophisticated gang member) or O.G. (original gangster) calling the shots and leading those youngsters astray. Veteranos and O.G.s are looked up to and are well respected among their peers. They make their money and get their power by utilizing young gang members to meet their agendas. All of these youngsters really think that they are doing something, when, in reality, they are being used, gobbled up, and thrown by the wayside.

Soldier on a mission . . .
Headed for prison . . .
Playing the game . . .
No one to blame . . .
© © ©
He decided to dance . . .
He took the chance . . .
Ready to war . . .
Now behind bars . . .
© © ©
Doing his time . . .
Toeing the line . . .
But he hasn't learned . . .
He just got turned . . .
© © ©
Straight up torpedo . . .
Gangster on the go . . .
At the direction of others . . .
Calls them his brothers . . .
© © ©
But it's really not so . . .
They use and they go . . .
Now the soldier's no good . . .
And even his hood . . .
© © ©
Puts him on shine . . .
Actions defined . . .
By a soldier gone bad . . .
Who's only been had . . .
© © ©
By those who abuse . . .
As they seek and they use . . .
Whoever they can . . .
To further their plan . . .
© © ©
Soldier on a mission . . .
The one that they're dissin' . . . !

"Miller (1992) defines a street gang as "a self-formed association of peers, united by mutual interests, with identifiable leadership and internal organization, who act collectively or as individuals to achieve specific purposes, including the conduct of illegal activity and control of a particular territory, facility, or enterprise." Miller, W.B. 1992 (Revised from 1982). Crime by Youth Gangs and Groups in the United States, Washington, DC: U.S. Department of Justice, Office of Justice Programs, Office of Juvenile Justice and Delinquency Prevention

In order to define the necessary strategies that are most effective in dealing with gangs, we first need to understand the structure of these gangs. This is very critical if we are to successfully deal with them, from the at-risk youth of our neighborhoods to the much more criminally sophisticated gang leaders. One cannot tend to something that one does not understand. Take a look at the Resource Guide provide below.

Information from the

GANG INTERVENTION PREVENTION and SUPPRESSION
Resource Guide

POLICY
Legislators, law enforcement, school administrators and parents recognize the far-reaching negative consequences of gang affiliation and crime. A zero tolerance for gang crime and activity is needed to immediately combat gang activity in our schools and community.

WHAT IS A GANG?
- On-going group
- Three or more members
- Common identifying sign or symbol (E.g. Red or Blue Clothing, XIII or XIV and Tattoos)
- The group's chief or primary occupation is the commission of certain, serious and violent felonies and;
- The group members have a pattern of committing serious and violent criminal activity. (California Penal Code Section 186.22)

WHY DO CHILDREN JOIN GANGS?
- Respect and status
- Peer Group
- Sense of belonging
- Peer pressure
- Low self-esteem
- Boredom
- Latest trends (clothing, music, etc.)
- Media
- Reaction to external racism
- Reaction to internal racism
- Environment
- Family tradition
- Neighborhood
- Association
- Protection

CONSEQUENCES OF GANG MEMBERSHIP
- Instant enemy to rival gangs
- Drug and alcohol abuse
- Drug dealing
- School failure
- Unemployment
- Incarceration
- Probation/Parole
- Home is marked by other gang members
- Family members victimized by rival gangs.
- Serious injury and/or lifetime disability
- Death

KEYS TO HELP PREVENT GANG MEMBERSHIP
- Apprehension, enforcement and abatements
- Education (Stay in school)
- Social/Community Based Organization (CBO) Services
- Positive feedback
- After-school activities
- Tattoo removal
- Parent/Guardian involvement

- High achievement
- Sports programming
- Teen support groups
- Diversion programs
- Teen pregnancy prevention
- Job placement/training services

Unless a child is born into or resides in a gang environment, there are many warning signals to their becoming susceptible to gang influence: poor school attendance, poor grades, school discipline referrals, lack of control/respect in the home, and home curfew violations. Who joins a youth gang? Enough studies have been done to give a composite picture. The typical youth gang member is a boy; some reports say more than 90 percent of gang members are male. His family is in the lower economic strata, he is not well educated, and has little promise of a lucrative or satisfying future. As he grows older, he feels a conflict between his own societal position and that of the middle class. In response to feelings of frustration and inadequacy, he takes risks, shows off, and demonstrates disdain for authority. He performs poorly in school and has little encouragement or support at home, where discipline is inconsistent. If it exists at all, it is likely to take the form of physical force. Unfortunately, this is the rule and many a disadvantaged youth do fall by the wayside. However, do not be fooled into thinking that because one is well off or comfortable economically, that one is exempt from the pull of gangs. I know many gang members who came from economically sound families.

WHAT PARENTS/FAMILIES/SCHOOLS CAN DO TO PREVENT GANGS?

- Know where your child is after school or in the evening
- Ask questions about school and friends
- Know your child's friends
- Visit the homes of your child's friend's parents
- Be active in your child's education
- Visit your child's school
- Meet on a regular basis with your child's teacher/counselor
- Establish a curfew for your child

- Be aware of gang clothing, tattoos or other paraphernalia
- Listen to your child
- Seek help from intervention services

WHAT CAN I DO IF MY CHILD JOINS A GANG?

- Immediately seek help from your child's school guidance counselor or police officer
- Set up a home visit with an intervention service provider
- Contact the district attorney's community prosecution unit or your local police agency
- Talk to your child about the consequences of a "Gangster lifestyle"
- Listen to your child to the top
- Encourage your child to succeed in school or after-school activities

WARNING SIGNS
CHILD

- Is truant or has failing grades
- Stays out late
- Admits to "Hanging out with kids in gangs"
- Shows a particular interest in a certain color/number
- Uses hand signal to communicate with friends
- Has specific gang drawings on school items
- Comes home with unexplained injuries or bruising
- Has unexplained cash/jewelry
- Carries a weapon or screwdriver
- Uses drugs or alcohol

CHAPTER FIVE

The warning signs

Secondly, we must understand our children. What makes them tick and why. What their ambitions are or if they even have any. We need to realize that many of their values lie in their unconscious mind. They are influenced by what they watch on television, what they hear or see in their lives, the music they listen to, and things that they have read. And most don't even realize this is happening. We need to awaken them to that reality. We need to be in tune with them and how they feel or think.

Young people join youth gangs for emotional and physical support. Feelings of frustration and inadequacy manifest themselves in dangerous acts, sometimes growing more dangerous as the gang members grow older. From petty theft, the youth turns to theft or assault with a weapon, often resulting in murder. In spite of the danger, and eventually because of it, these troubled young people find reward and status in the youth gang that they cannot get at home or in school. I know that personally, I loved the attention and sense of false respect that I got from acting out in the type of behavior relative to gang association. It just made me feel good and gave me a defiled sense of worth.

Not all those who display the outward signs of gang membership are actually involved in illegal gang activity. We must remember that the way of dress in many of today's youth is an echo of the gang culture that is espoused through the various media. It's just the way they dress, so particular attention must be paid to every child with regard to gang activity. That is not to say that they are not being exposed to, or are being influenced by, or are passively involved in the peripheral edges of gang activity, because many kids today are. An individual's age, physical structure, ability to fight, tattoos, willingness to use violence, and arrest record are most often the principal factors that determine where an individual stands within the gang hierarchy.

A gang's structure can vary depending on the size which can be as small as a group of five or ten to several hundred or several thousand members. Many of the larger gangs will break up into smaller factions with loyalties toward the larger structure, yet having a hierarchy of their own within the group. These smaller factions spread and grow, bringing more territory and power to the larger group as they expand and recruit new members. A good example would be the Norteno gang. It has several thousand members all across Northern California, but each neighborhood faction is an independent unit with ties to the larger group. Most minor gangs operate informally with leadership falling to whoever takes control; others have distinct leadership and are highly structured, much like business or corporation and delegate duties and roles to their subordinate members in specific areas with specific goals in mind.

Some have argued that increasing gang activity is directly related to decreases in adult mentors, school failures, decreases in after-school programs and similar failures by the adults in the lives of children. But it is my belief that government involvement that dictates how we should discipline our children is also partially to blame. How schools should maintain discipline has quite a bit to do with it as well. Because of laws enacted currently, parents and educators are forbidden to effectively discipline their charges. Children receive no direct penalties for their actions any more.

While kids from more affluent neighborhoods may turn to other less dangerous alternatives, children from poorer neighborhoods often turn to gangs, both as a protection and a place to find love and understanding. It starts from the little guy just starting out as a "wanna be", all the way up to the gang leaders who reside in prison and call the shots and it is a progression in criminal behavior and attitude. I went from a "wanna be" neighborhood thug to becoming a member of one of America's most infamous and violent prison gangs.

Only those peripheral players who are just beginning to identify with the gangs and gang culture are reachable. I stopped being reachable at about twelve years old. That was the very first time I went to reform school. From that point on, I became incorrigible and no one could tell me anything . . . I knew it all! I was the tough neighborhood thug who just came out of reform school . . . and I had my respect . . . and wasn't ready to give that up. Just like I was, the rest are already anarchists and anti-authority individuals. They are past listening and have to learn the hard way, like I did. They bring misery to their parents, family, and community and really don't care about anyone, not even themselves. We need to focus on stopping the transition from "wanna be" to that level of involvement. And that level starts pretty early, as in my case.

Kids in that age range should be thinking about the latest comic book or the newest toy out on the market, and somewhere along the lines of modern society we lost that innocence. Kids now days look to the latest rap stars or Hollywood thugs for inspiration. They would rather emulate them than act like kids. Or they are lost in the violence of the latest video game which espouses violence, crime, and sexual immorality. They grow up too fast. Innocence is what we need to strive to bring back and instill in these potential "wanna be's".

Matthew O'Deane, Ph.D., has identified five primary steps of gang involvement applicable to the majority of gangs in the world; at risk, associates, members, hardcore members and leaders.

Step one is "At Risk" or "Peripheral"

These kids are not considered gang members by law enforcement, but they know gang members and may associate with them on a casual or limited basis, mostly watching and imitating the older gang members. They are getting close to an age where they might decide to join the gang. They may like and admire the gang members in the neighborhood and the gang lifestyle, but do not participate in the gang's criminal activity. This group is generally between 7 and 9 years old, but can range from 5 to 16 years old in some cases; this group should be the primary target of gang prevention programs. Many kids in this classification choose alternatives to the gang life and never join a gang. The key is to feed off of those successes and replicate the positive results in the areas that have the largest concentration of at-risk youth.

Step two is "Associates" or "Affiliates"

These kids associate with gang members on a regular basis and tend to consider gang life normal and acceptable. They find certain things in common with gang members and are seriously thinking about joining the gang. Some associates consider themselves members, even if they have not yet been formally initiated. This person is commonly called a "Wanna Be", "Pee Wee", "Baby Gangster" or "Tiny Gangster"; many may claim to back up the gang if confronted by law enforcement. They may act like, walk like, talk like, and dress like gang members and will tend to socialize with them. These associates are sometimes used by older gang members to do specific tasks, such as serving as lookouts, runners, or for writing graffiti. This group typically lacks direction and may drift in and out of the gang depending on the current activities of the gang. This person is generally between the ages of 9 and 13, but can range from 7 to 18 years old in some cases. It is often times difficult to distinguish an associate from a member by looking at them. The difference is in their commitment to the gang.

Step three is the "Gang member"

This person associates almost exclusively with other gang members to the exclusion of family and former friends. They have shifted their loyalty from their family to their gang. This person participates in gang crimes and most of the gang's activities. They make up the bulk of a gang's membership and are held responsible for protection of the gangs turf and fellow gang members. This person is generally between the ages of 14 and 20 years old, but can range from 11 to 40 years old in some cases. The gang member has a much more significant attachment to the gang mentality or code when compared to an associate.

Step four is the "Hard Core Gang Member"

This gang member has become totally committed to the gang and gang lifestyle, commonly referred to as an "OG" or Original Gangster or "Veterano." They usually reject any value system other than that of his/her or her gang and his or her life revolves around the gang. This member typically has been arrested and been through the justice system. This person will commit any crime or act of violence to further the goals and objectives of the gang. This person is usually in his or her late teens or early 20s extending into his or her 30s in some cases.

Step five is the *"Gang Leader"*

These members are the upper echelons of the gang's command. This gang member is probably the oldest in the group and likely has an extensive criminal record and he or she often have the power to direct the gang's activity, whether he or she is involved or not. In many jurisdictions, this person is likely a prison gang member calling the shots from within the prison system or is on parole. Sometimes times they distance themselves from the street gang activities and make attempts to appear legitimate, possibly operating a business that they run as fronts for the gang's drug dealing or other illegal operations.

CHAPTER SIX

Prison gangs

"The 2005 study neither War nor Peace: International Comparisons of Children and Youth in Organized Armed Violence studied ten cities worldwide and found that in eight of them, "street gangs had strong links to prison gangs."
**Luke Dowdney - Children in Organized and Armed Violence
(COAV) | 5/31/2005**

Prison gangs are groups in a prison or correctional institution setting that have formed for mutual protection, power, and advancement. They control prison yards and most illegal activities that go on within the prison setting, but their focus is on money and power. So more often than not, prison gangs have several "affiliates" or "chapters" in different state prison systems that branch out due to the movement or transfer of their members. They also have subordinate groups within the prison system and the streets. Their influence is ever growing and all-encompassing, and their target is usually the at-risk youths who are looking for an identity and someone or something to belong to.

I know that part of my training within the gang I belonged to was to get ready for an eventual entry into street level criminal activities. It was what we aspired to as that is where the real money is. Each one of us was educated in the workings of regimental operations within the streets. The focus is on the money and loyalty to the gang. The education was sophisticated, carefully thought out, and meant as a way for our group to enter the streets and make as much money as possible, regardless of the consequences or the collateral damage it may bring with it.

Although the majority of gang leaders from Chicago are now incarcerated, as are most of the country's other prison gang leaders (some in the most secure federal prison in the country, Florence, Colorado's ADX), most of those leaders continue to manage their gangs from within prison. It's an ongoing process that never stops. Penal institutions have long sought to minimize the power and influence of gang leaders by isolating them from other inmates and limiting their outside contact, but it has been a wasted effort, as they continue to communicate and wreak havoc in general population settings and on the streets of America.

As easily as they are removed from a general population setting, others step up to resume the responsibilities left by the vacancy, and the person removed moves up in rank. The leadership doesn't usually change . . . only the players do . . . because they are expendable. Take note further in this book that the five generals of the Nuestra Familia were removed from the state prison system and sent to the federal ADX facility and a new general David (DC) Cervantes set himself up as the sole leader of the gang by demoting those who threatened his authority, and vacating the authority of the exiting Generals.

The reality is that criminal gangs do function inside and outside of prisons, such as the Mexican Mafia, La Nuestra Familia, and the Aryan Brotherhood. During the 1970s, prison gangs in California began recruiting street gang members from outside to increase associations between prison and street gangs, and as a consolidation of power in particular California geographical areas. Like the Nuestra Familia recruiting in Northern California, and the Mexican Mafia recruiting in Southern California.

In the United States most prison gangs are in organized crime inside of prisons such as extortion, drugs, and gambling, and outside of prisons, running drugs, and committing mayhem and murder. Take a minute and read about **"Operation Black Widow,"** a F.B.I. task force operation involving several law enforcement agencies targeting the illegal street activities of La Nuestra Familia, The Northern Structure, and the Norteno gang. Their power and influences were far-reaching and extensive in all Northern California cities. The FBI task-force, dubbed "Black Widow", was the largest investigation into prison gang activities in California's history. It soon became a multi agency endeavor, including the FBI, the California Department of Corrections, and the US attorney, operating out of their command center at a downtown high-rise in Santa Rosa.

Operation Black Widow

"The U.S. Department of Justice's costliest and longest investigation of a California prison gang came to a quiet close Monday as top Nuestra Familia leaders pleaded guilty to criminal racketeering charges in a San Francisco courtroom."

"The multi-agency, multimillion-dollar prosecution started in 2000 with the indictment of Salinas Nuestra Familia members Hector Gallegos, Caesar Ramirez, Rico Garcia and others by U.S. Attorney Robert Mueller, now director of the Federal Bureau of Investigation."

"The pleas bring an end to Operation Black Widow, a controversial investigation that began in 1997 and aimed to break the leadership of the Nuestra Familia, the notorious prison gang with extensive operations in Salinas."

"The FBI was the lead investigative agency in the operation that involved nearly 30 federal, state and local law enforcement agencies, including the Monterey County District Attorney's office and Salinas police. Seventy-five people have been prosecuted as part of Operation Black Widow and spin-off state and federal prosecutions, said U.S. Attorney Steven Gruel."

"Eight Nuestra Familia gang leaders agreed to prison sentences Monday in federal court. Five men agreed to federal life sentences and another three agreed to 10 years in federal custody."

"The goal of the prosecution, said federal Judge Charles Breyer, was to take the gang's leadership out of California's prisons and "disperse them to the four corners of federal jurisdiction."

"I am no expert but I hope that the federal Bureau of Prisons will be able to curtail or eliminate the level of gang activity," Breyer said."

"With the pre-trial guilty pleas, the organization and inner workings of the upper echelon of the Nuestra Familia will not be brought to public light in a jury trial. It also means that the integrity of the government's informant, Danny Hernandez, one of the highest ranked criminals ever to cooperate with the FBI, will not be questioned by federal defense attorneys."

"Gerald Rubalcaba, Cornelio Tristan, James Morado, Tex Hernandez and Joseph Hernandez, all of whom are currently serving life sentences in state prison, agreed to life in federal custody. A global settlement allowed for 10-year federal sentences for Henry Cervantes, Daniel Perez and Alberto Larez, a former Salinas resident. Gruel said the defendants have all been in and out of prison since 1979."

"All defendants pleaded guilty to one count of criminal racketeering, which Gruel said included conspiracy and murder, specifically the 1998 Salinas murders of Michael "Mikeo" Castillo and Vincent Garcia-Sanchez."

"By 2001, 22 members and associates of the Nuestra Familia were indicted on more than 30 charges including murder, racketeering, assault, drug trafficking and conspiracy. It was the last major investigation led by Robert Mueller before he was picked to head the FBI. By last November, 13 of the defendants had pleaded guilty. On July 21, the only defendant facing the death penalty, Rico Garcia, of Salinas, pleaded guilty and agreed to a federal life sentence."

"It remains to be seen ultimately whether this prosecution was warranted in the long run," Breyer said. Acknowledging the possible risk of introducing prison gang leaders into the federal prison system, he added, "This disposition is the only one that makes sense."

"The case has been controversial in part because the leading government informant, Hernandez, was found to have engaged in unauthorized criminal activity while under the FBI's watch, including gun trafficking and drug dealing. Lawyers involved in

*the case also have contended that Hernandez ordered the May 2001
execution of Raymond Sanchez at Cap's Saloon in Salinas."*

*"Prosecutor Gruel said the pleas entered Monday were conditional
and dependent on the defendants' state sentences being commuted
by the California Department of Corrections, Gov. Schwarzenegger
and the state Supreme Court. Federal defense attorneys expect
the state sentences to be commuted by early December, when the
defendants' new federal sentences will be handed down."*

Freelance reporter Julia Reynolds contributed to this article

Those ruling members of La Nuestra Familia left vacancies in the
California Prison System's prison gang, which have already been filled by
a deadlier type of leadership. One man has emerged as the sole General
and leader of the Nuestra Familia. Two other possible candidates have
already been dealt with by this new leader and have been stripped of
their authority and are now low category members. That is just the way
it works in their world. It's survival of the deadliest and most powerful
members. Take off one head and another grows, and sometimes the next
head is even deadlier. This new leader is not about to allow anyone to
share his ultimate authority.

> *The color of blood . . .*
> *The color of creation.*
> *Stained with the mud . . .*
> *Of gang indoctrination.*
> ©©©
> *When does it stop?*
> *Is there a cure?*
> *So far it's a flop . . .*
> *Breeding hatred so pure.*
> ©©©
> *Yet silently they go . . .*
> *Into the game.*
> *Fortune their goal . . .*
> *Seeking their fame.*
> ©©©

Not knowing the cost . . .
Or even the rules.
Soon they are lost . . .
A menagerie of fools.
©©©
Killing and dying.
Whatever for?
Thieving and lying . . .
Is all that's in store.
©©©
We must break free . . .
Of this social disease.
Then we can be . . .
Alive and in peace!
©©©

Aryan-Brotherhood

The Aryan Brotherhood, also known as The Brand, the AB, or the One-Two, is a white prison gang and organized crime syndicate in the United States with about 19,000 members in and out of prison. According to the Federal Bureau of Investigation (FBI), although the gang makes up less than 1% of the prison population, it is responsible for up to 21% of murders in the federal prison system. The AB has focused on the economic activities typical of organized crime entities, particularly drug trafficking, extortion, inmate prostitution, and murder-for-hire.

Organization at lower levels varies from prison to prison. For example, in the Arizona prison system, members are known as "kindred" and organize into "families". A "council" controls the families. Kindred may recruit other members, known as "progeny", and serve as a mentor for the new recruit. The group has an alliance with La Eme (The Mexican Mafia) as the two are mutual enemies of Black Guerilla Family. According to a federal indictment, the AB has partnered with Asian gangs to import heroin from Thailand.

Like most prison gangs, Aryan Brotherhood members mark themselves with distinctive tattoos. Designs commonly include the words "Aryan Brotherhood", "AB", SS, 666, sig runes, shamrocks, and other Nazi symbolism and Celtic iconography. The Aryan Brotherhood, now a potent force in prisons across the United States, began in 1967, in California's notorious San Quentin State Prison. They have spread across the country in state and federal prisons with their federal headquarters based it the ADX Federal Super-max Prison.

The Aryan Brotherhood are rivals of the gang I belonged to because of their alliance with the Mexican Mafia and their subsequent attack and murder of an NF member at the behest of the Mexican Mafia. On February 3, 1972, Aryan Brotherhood members murder Nuestra familia member Fred Charles Castillo. Because of this alliance between the two the Nuestra Familia/Nuestra Raza/Norteno group had an uneasy relationship with most whites. We were allowed to do business with only the Northern California based biker groups because they had their own issues with the Aryan Brotherhood. We also had an uneasy alliance with the Sacramaniacs gang formed in the Sacramento County jail system (a predominantly Norteno jail system), because they were also at odds with the Aryan Brotherhood as well. Currently the NF/NR/Norteno regime is at war with all whites regardless of their background.

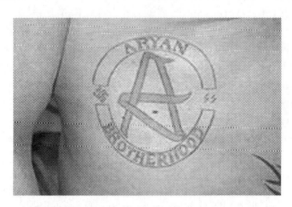

Aryan Brotherhood member's tattoo.

In late 2002, over 40 leaders of the gang were simultaneously rounded up from prisons all over the country and brought to trial under the Racketeer Influenced and Corrupt Organizations

Act (RICO) among them was Mr. Dustin (Mickey Mouse) D., a fearsome member known to visit Disneyland a lot. The intention was to bring death sentences for at least 21 of them, to cut off the leadership of the gang, in a manner similar to tactics used against organized crime. The case produced 30 convictions but none of the most powerful leaders received a death sentence. Sentencing occurred in March 2006 for three of the most powerful leaders of the gang, including Barry Byron Mills (born 1948) and AB "lieutenant" Tyler "The Hulk" Bingham, who were indicted for numerous crimes, including murder, conspiracy, drug trafficking, and racketeering and for ordering killings and beatings from their cell. Bingham and Mills were convicted of murder and sent back to United States Penitentiary Administrative Maximum Facility Prison (ADX) in Florence, Colorado where they are serving life sentences with no parole, escaping the death penalty.

Prosecuting the gang has been historically difficult, because many members are already serving life sentences with no possibility of parole, so prosecutors were seeking the death penalty for 21 of those indicted but have dropped the death penalty on all but five defendants. By September 2006, the 19 inductees not eligible for the death penalty had pled guilty. The first of a series of trials involving four high level members ended in convictions in July 2006. On 23 June 2005, after a 20-month investigation, a federal strike force raided six houses in northeastern Ohio belonging to the "Order of the Blood", a criminal organization controlled by the Aryan Brotherhood. Thirty-four Aryan Brotherhood members or associates were arrested and warrants were issued for ten more. Since 1979, Aryan Nations has been engaged in prison outreach. This is an important aspect of the Aryan Nations' agenda, given that so many members of The Order and Aryan Nations are now serving long prison sentences. Aryan Nations corresponds on an ongoing basis with prison inmates through letters and the forwarding of its periodicals. In 1987, Aryan Nations began publishing a "prison outreach newsletter" called The Way, which has facilitated recruitment and connections between Aryan Nations and its offspring, Aryan Brotherhood, a network of prison gang members.

Black-Guerilla-Family

Like the Aryan Brotherhood after them, the Black Guerilla Family formed in San Quentin Penitentiary in 1966. They have remained a constant threat to the California Prison System and have ties to the KUMI nation. The Black Guerrilla Family (also known as the Black Family or the Black Vanguard) is a prison gang founded in 1966 by George Jackson and W.L. Nolen while they were incarcerated at San Quentin State Prison in Marin County, California, north of San Francisco. The BGF was founded with the stated goals of eradicating racism, maintaining dignity in prison, and overthrowing the United States government.

BGF was associated with a number of leftist groups, including the Black Liberation Army, Symbionese Liberation Army, and Weather Underground. The group is strongly organized on both the East and West coasts, and cooperates with the Nuestra Familia, Latin Kings, the Bloods, and the Crips. Both Mexican Mafia and Aryan Brotherhood consider Black Guerilla Family to be their main rival. Ten people reputedly BGF members were indicted in July, 2010 in Baltimore, Maryland including a prison guard for various crimes committed in prison and on the streets.

Huey P. Newton murder

On August 22, 1989, co-founder and leader of the <u>Black Panther Party for Self Defense</u>, <u>Huey P. Newton</u> was fatally shot on the 1400 block of 9th street in <u>West Oakland</u> by 24-year-old Black Guerilla Family member, Tyrone Robinson. Robinson was convicted of the murder in August 1991 and sentenced to 32 years for the crime. Official accounts claimed that the killer was a known drug dealer in Oakland. Robinson contended that Newton pulled a gun when the two met at a street corner in the neighborhood, Sergeant Mercado said, but investigators said they found no evidence Newton had been armed. The killing occurred in a very neighborhood where Newton, years earlier as minister of defense for the Black Panthers, once set up social programs that helped destitute Blacks. Newton's last words, as he stood facing his killer, were, "You can kill my body, but you can't kill my soul. My soul will live forever!" He was then shot three times in the face by Robinson, who went by the street name "Double R".

I happened to know "Double R" very well. We grew up together in the prison system. He was a 415 (Bay Area gang member) and I was a Norteno and at that time we were the strongest of allies in the turf wars of the California Prison Yards. We dealt drugs and worked with one another in an effort to keep control of the prison where we were housed at. I remember when he went home and shot Huey Newton. That was how "Double R' made his bones and entry into the much bigger and more violent Black Guerrilla Family. The 415's were to the BGF like the Nortenos were to the Nuestra Familia.

Fresno Bulldogs

Because of this push for power by "Black Bob" the Nuestra Familia was split in two with many taking either "Black Bob's" side or "Babo" Sosa's side. The result was a parting of the group into what is now known as the "Bulldogs".

This Security Threat Group started from the Fresno 14 Gang (F-14) on the street combined with inmate elements at San Quentin Prison in the early 1980's who called themselves Bulldogs after the Fresno State University mascot. At one time the F14 were aligned with the Nuestra Familia and Nortenos. They still will often wear red and sometimes have dog paw tattoos, but are now independent from other Nortenos or Nor. Cal. They will fight Surenos, Nortenos and other gangs and seldom get along with anybody. They will often bark as a call sign, call each other "DOGS", and are sometimes found outside of the Fresno, CA area.

ᵀᴴᴱ COLLEGIAN

November 16, 2005 California State University, Fresno

Editorial: Policing of gang activity not effective

"Sting and run: that's Fresno's police strategy to rid the city of gang activity. The Fresno police department has dropped the ball when it comes to regulating gangs around the city of Fresno."

"Two factors that contribute to the increase of gang activity in Fresno are poverty and the lack of a permanent police presence. It is not unrealistic to see a connection between the recent gang violence in Fresno and the city's ranking as having the highest poverty concentration in the nation. According to the 2000 census, 60,000 of nearly 800,000 Fresnans lived in high poverty neighborhoods between 1990 and 2000."

"A report from the Brookings Research Institution shows Fresno with a concentrated poverty rate of 43.5 percent. The report indicates that a concentrated poverty rate reflected the proportion of poor people citywide who live in extreme poverty neighborhoods. Poverty in certain areas of the city serves as a great source for gang members to recruit young people."

"Although Fresno police frequent these areas they are not a permanent presence. This has resulted in the escalation of violence over the past few years and shows the methods used to control gangs are no longer effective. Meshing police into the neighborhood landscape is a surefire way to keep gang activity down."

"A perfect example is the police substation located in El Dorado Park, near Bulldog Stadium. For more than three years the police

have served this area and have seen a significant decrease in gang violence and crime."

"Yes, crime still exists. A consistent police presence serves as a reminder to would-be criminals and serves as a comfort to residents."

"Fresno Police should follow the same pattern for the rest of the city. In areas such as West Fresno, which has the most concentrated areas of gang violence, police need to reestablish their presence. This ensures criminal activities don't take root and allows the police to regulate the current activity with a hands-on approach, not third person through 911 call centers. Police need to build a substation within one of these neighborhoods. Although the occasional stings result in high numbers in arrests, firearms and narcotics recovered, think of the returns if the department was a part of the permanent landscape. Police should not be waiting until people die before they put together an operation to quell the violence."

"The city should also get involved in improving rundown neighborhoods. Most of the gang-infested areas are the ones neglected by the city. The houses are rundown with little access to amenities such as parks, health centers and schools. Five gang-related deaths have occurred in the past month and this should be enough to show city officials this is a serious problem in need of much more than just temporary supervision."

"Of course, city leaders are taking notice, according to an article on the ABC30 Web site, "their overall plan to combat gang violence is having a no tolerance policy and to reach out to at-risk youth. Although the plan sounds encouraging, such things cannot happen if the problem is not addressed at the root, further highlighting the unnecessary act of implementing police presence in short spurts."

"What is really needed is a more constant sense of security for civilians. A constant police presence would also create a sense of authority that might deter gang members from committing

petty crime. More surveillance could prevent petty crimes from escalating into bigger, uncontrollable acts."

"It seems like the city is choosing to ignore neglected neighborhoods when they should be encouraging programs to revitalize the community such as Big Brothers, Big Sister and other mentoring programs. The problem is ongoing so the solution should be as well. The problem will never be fixed but small steps toward emphasizing the concept of "community" instead of "gangs" will give young people a sense of involvement that is positive to themselves and the people around them."
http://www.csufresno.edu/Collegian/archive/2005/11

ⓒⓒⓒ
Gangster stares . . .
And rival glares.
What's it about?
You wanna shout!
ⓒⓒⓒ
Why do they hate?
Is it too late?
Flamed up in red . . .
Already dead.
ⓒⓒⓒ
Just unaware . . .
That they are headed there.
Too young for a grave . . .
Trying to be brave.
ⓒⓒⓒ
Just to impress . . .
Those who care less.
But do they know?
They've given their soul.
ⓒⓒⓒ
For something that's fake.
Just there to take . . .
Their life and their blood.
Not any good.

It's really all bad.
Makes you so sad . . .
That nothing you'll do
Will make their heart true.

Texas-Syndicate

The Texas Syndicate (or Syndicato Tejano) is a mostly Texas-based prison gang that includes Hispanic and at one time, White members. The Texas Syndicate, unlike La Eme or Nuestra Familia, has been more associated or allied with Mexican immigrant prisoners, known as "border brothers", while La Eme and the NF tend to be more composed of US-born/raised Hispanics. It was established in the 1960s at Folsom Prison in California in direct response to the other California prison gangs (notably the Aryan Brotherhood and Mexican Mafia), which were attempting to prey on native Texas inmates. Los Zetas cartel has been known to hire US gangs such as the Texas Syndicate and MS-13 to carry out contract killings.

Jamiyyat Ul Islam Is Saheeh

Jamiyyat Ul Islam Is Saheeh was allegedly formed in the California Correctional Institution in Tehachapi, as an offshoot of the Nation of Islam, led by Louis Farrakhan, one of the largest Muslim religious sects in American prisons.

Mexican-Mafia

The Mexican Mafia was formed in 1957 by Mexican street gang members incarcerated at the Deuel Vocational Institution, a state prison located in Tracy, California. The founder of the gang was Luis "Huero Buff" Flores, who was previously a member of the Hawaiian Gardens gang.

Mexican Mafia: Prison Gang Profile
by insideprison.com, May 2006

"One of the first prison gangs to develop in the United States, the Mexican Mafia began in 1957 in California. In 1993, San Antonio FBI Special Agent-in-Charge Jeff Jamar called El Eme, often now the name given to the gang on the street, "the most dominant of the prison-spawned gangs operating in Texas," when comparing it to the 10 other large-scale gangs active in US prisons at the time. In 1992, membership within prison was hovering at 700, while in 1998 it was just under 1,500. Today it continues to rise. Outside of prison, La EME is still an ominous presence, responsible for 10% of San Antonio"s total homicide rate, with thousands of members estimated to be operating across the United States."

"While California and Texas prisons house high numbers of both the California branch and Texas branch of the Mexican Mafia, the two states' respective prison gangs are not officially linked. While they both operate by the same broad title, the Texas branch identifies itself as "Mexikanemi," (Soldiers of Aztlan), or La EMI, while the California branch identifies itself as La EME. In addition, southern California's branch of the Mexican Mafia calls itself the Surenos (or Sur-13), as opposed to the Nuestra Familia's subdivision in northern California, the Nortenos."

"The Texas chapter of the Mexican Mafia was founded in a Huntsville prison in 1984 by Heriberto "Herbie" Huerta. Huerta was serving three life terms for murder conspiracy and racketeering when he was given permission by the California chapter to establish his own branch in Texas. Huerta also wrote the constitution that is followed by members to this day, and continues to collect and manage revenue generated by criminal activities. Huerta's prison bank account held $8,000 in 2002, the result of a 10% tax called the "dime" that is collected by drug earnings made on Mexican Mafia turf on the outside."

Objectives

"As a previous spiritual leader of the Mexikanemi Science Temple of Aztlan, Huerta followed a pre-Hispanic creed that related his desire to establish a legitimate network built on "character," and an emphasis of love over hate. However, the actual objective of the Mexican Mafia is to earn money through criminal operations. The Mexican Mafia's Constitution, which outlines all aspects of criminal organization and enterprising, was recently described in the San Antonio Express-News, citing a prosecution's address to the jury during a 2005 trial: "the Mexican Mafia is a 'criminal organization' that works 'in any criminal aspect or interest for the benefit and advancement of Mexikanemi. We shall deal in drugs, contract killings, prostitution, large-scale robbery, gambling, weapons and everything imaginable." It goes on to declare that the only punishment approved by the organization is death."

Location

"The Mexican Mafia's headquarters are located in San Antonio, but its members reach across several jurisdictions, including California, Arizona, Corpus Christi, El Paso, Houston, Dallas, and Midwestern and southern Texas."

Structure and Organization

"According to law enforcement, the Mexican Mafia follows a strict hierarchy and a rigid set of "by-laws." The organization has a written constitution outlining all aspects of its criminal organization and enterprising. As covered in the San Antonio Express-News, citing a 2005 trial, the Mexican Mafia "shall deal in drugs, contract killings, prostitution, large-scale robbery, gambling, weapons and everything imaginable." The constitution also stipulates, as most prison gangs do today, that gang members released from prison become "free world soldiers" required to serve the gang's economic interest by dealing in drugs, racketeering, and prostitution on the outside. These recent parolees, generally termed "wolfpacks" by both the Mexican Mafia and the Nuestra Familia, carry messages to gang leaders on the outside."

According to Robert Fong (1990), the Mafia's Constitution outlines 12 principal rules.
Membership is for life, meaning "blood in, blood out."

Every member must be prepared to sacrifice his life or take another's life at any time when required

Every member shall strive to overcome his weakness to achieve discipline within the MEXIKANEMI brotherhood

Never let the MEXIKANEMI down
"The sponsoring member is totally responsible for the behavior of the new recruit. If the new recruit turns out to be a traitor, it is the sponsoring member's responsibility to eliminate the recruit."

When disrespected by a stranger or a group, all members of the MEXIKANEMI will unite to destroy the person or the other group completely.

Always maintain a high level of integrity.

Never release the MEXIKANEMI business to others.

Every member has the right to express opinions, ideas, contradictions and constructive Criticisms.

Every member has the right to organize, educate, arm, and defend the MEXIKANEMI.

Every member has the right to wear the tattoo of the MEXIKANEMI symbol
The MEXIKANEMI is a criminal organization and therefore will participate in all aspects of criminal interest for monetary benefits (Constitution of the Mexican Mafia of Texas).

"The Mexican Mafia operates on a paramilitary structure, complete with a president, vice president, and numerous generals, captains, lieutenants and sergeants. Below these high-ranking members

are soldiers, also known as "carnales," as well as suppliers and
associates, all of whose activities are overseen by the generals. Only
one general operates in the federal prison system, while another one
operates in the state prison system. The state general appoints a
committee of lieutenants and captains who command prison units
across the entire state."
http://www.insideprison.com/mexican-mafia-prison-gang.asp

Neta-Association

Some reports claim Neta originated in 1980, while others claim it
was founded earlier, perhaps in the 1970s sometime. It was originally
founded in Oso Blanco Prison, Rio Piedras, Puerto Rico, then also
known as "Asociacion Pro-Derecho Al Confinando." It then spread to
New York, New Jersey and Connecticut.

Nortenos (XIV)

A loose knit group of Hispanics from Northern California cities
who identify with La Nuestra Familia and La Nuestra Raza prison
gangs and are a recruitment ground for these gangs. Most nortenos will
be recruited into the Nuestra Raza (Northern Structure) by recruiters
who are trained to do so. Once in the NR it is a natural progression to
move up into the ranks of La Nuestra Familia. However, this can only
be done by sponsorship by a made member. La Nuestra Raza requires
mandatory commitment inside of prison and a choice to commit
outside of prison, while La Nuestra Familia is a mandatory lifetime
commitment. Blood in, blood out.

The Nortenos Gang—History and Culture

Nortenos are those gang members that come from all northern
California cities and towns with the exception of Fresno and
surrounding towns. The dividing line between north and south is
Bakersfield. This gang has its roots in the California Department

of Corrections and is associated with both the Nuestra familia and the Nuestra Raza. This association began around 1960 when the CDCR prison inmates began to identify by northern and southern California. Nortenos have become bitter rivals of the sureno factions and the Mexican Mafia. This rivalry was started when a member of the Mexican Mafia stole a nortenos shoes and they became sworn enemies.

Nortenos have been involved with organized crime through their association with the NF and NR. Illegal acts like drug trafficking, murder, and armed conflict are trademarks of the Norteno gang member. Nortenos are highly organized and have a militaristic outlook on things. They are highly disciplined, in excellent physical shape, and very dangerous. They have a rigid command structure and a very involved chain of command (COC). One black inmate I knew told me that we reminded him of a pack of rabid pit bulls because someone was constantly getting stabbed or assaulted. Norftenos exist in every state in America and abroad in Europe as well. The Nortenos are unified, keeping them one of the most powerful and threatening gangs in California. A list of the Nortenos laws was found by police in a prison. It includes provisions against drug and alcohol abuse, as well as homosexual activity, and discusses duties and required hours of attention."

Members will wear signifying colors or apparel to flaunt who they are and as a challenge to others. The color red, the number fourteen, XIV, X4, ene, Aztec art work, four dots, the five point star, or the huelga bird are all signifiers of the norteno gang. The last two must be earned before a norteno can put it on him. This usually requires a hit. Many wear San Francisco Forty-Niners apparel, Raiders apparel, BK's or K-Swiss tennis shoes. They were their hair in a Mongolian top knot (as of recent they have seemed to shy away from that signifier) or a fade. Though the Nortenos have been unsuccessful in gaining any territory past the Delano dividing line, the Surenos have gained ground in the north. The difficulties of the Nortenos in this area speak to the gang density in the South, where the number of Surenos in Los Angeles outnumbers Crips and Bloods combined. However, the Nortenos still remain one of the most famous and dangerous gangs in the United States.

Symbols of the Nuestra Familia, Nuestra Raza, and Norteno gangs. http://www.improve247.com/society/the-nortenos-gang-history-and-culture#home

Nuestra-Familia

La Nuestra Familia was formed in San Quentin State Prison around 1968, constructed as a force that could combat the existing oppression of the dominant Mexican Mafia. Once formed and consolidated in power the Nuestra Familia moved across California's prison yards, across all of Northern California, and eastward across the United States and developed prominent ties in Colorado state prisons, as Nuestra Familia members were incarcerated there and formed a new chapter.

Today La Nuestra Familia has moved into the federal prison system in the wake of the Black Widow indictments and subsequent convictions. As of this writing the previous leadership of the Nuestra Familia (La Mesa) and several high ranking members were sent to the federal prison system under a plea deal with prosecutors. The top five generals were sent to the ADX Maximum Security Penitentiary and others were sent to various federal prisons. It is still to be seen what affect that will have on any possible expansion of the NF. If expansion does occur, it will most likely be another chapter of the NF as in the Colorado prison system, as those who went to the federal system were stripped of their authority within the California chapter by the new leading regime, although some members have continued to stay loyal to the previous regime. Because of this, there exists a rift among the rank and file of La Nuestra Familia.

The Nuestra Familia, operates as a "mutual aid society," committed to providing commissary goods to fellow Familia members, Nuestra Raza members, and Norteno gang members in prison at inexpensive or "face value" costs, and providing commissary goods to members placed in administrative segregation. This is how they look out for their own, and is done so that those who follow them can feel that they count for something. They also offer unlimited protection to those who commit to their agenda. They maintain an "all for one, one for all" attitude with regard to any opposition. To assault, move on (stab), or otherwise cross a made member of La Nuestra Familia or La Nuestra Raza results in a "greenlight" (order to assault, stab, or kill) being placed on the aggressor.

The real deal is that they are a "militaristic" entity whose primary concern is the making of money and the seeking of power for those who rule the roost. And they accomplish this through murder and intimidation. They kill quickly, without provocation, and they kill ruthlessly. They are what they are and they make no bones about it. In the last three decades the NF/NR/Norteno faction have been the most aggressive and violent faction within the California Prison system. They declared war on the Fresno Bulldogs, all whites, the EME and the Surenos, the California Correctional Officers, and some black inmate factions. They run an Ad-Seg yard with militaristic ruthlessness and discipline, allowing only those whom they deem fit to be in their presence. Anyone else is assaulted and removed quickly.

The Nuestra Familia strives to protect and preserve Chicano culture even in the face of brutal violence expended on their part both in California and Colorado prisons. Aztec history and NF history are mandatory subjects of study for all members as are "The Art of War" by Sun Tzu, and other war strategy writings. They do this to instill a war readiness attitude among the rank and file. In furtherance of that attitude all N.F. members, N.R. members, and Norteno gang members are required to commit to a daily regimen of cardio exercise called La Maquina" (the machine). This exercise regimen consists mainly of burpees (an extreme cardio push-up from a standing position) and intense cardio-calisthenics. To not participate in the machine is not accepted and a chronic violator will be dealt with accordingly.

The Nuestra Familia operates with a "cause" or an ideology that places great emphasis on the psychological and physical protection of its members as well as the preservation of the Nuestra Familia culture itself, in and out of prisons. They preach a false sense of honor, pride, and integrity as part of their social make-up. They believe that they are an honorable organization and will go to any lengths to protect the integrity of their group. Because of this La Nuestra Familia is continually cleaning up its ranks and ridding itself of what it labels as "degenerates" or "bandidos". A degenerate is one who works with the K-9 and infoms on the group, or is a member drop-out. A bandido is one who speaks out against the group and their agenda. The NF has a hit list that is called the BNL or Bad News List. This list is well over a thousand names long. I imagine that I am somewhere on that list.

In 1997 an FBI investigation revealed that top-ranking Nuestra Familia leaders were creating new recruits and turning them into organized criminal operatives upon release, also known as "regiments", governed by released NF members. From their thrones in California's Pelican Bay State Prison, they controlled the intra-prison drug trade, while communicating with their members on the outside, ordering hits and organizing drug smuggling rings and local street cartels. The severe isolation of the maximum control unit was not nearly enough to stop the flow of information and orders emanating from there to all other prisons and to the street regiments.

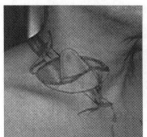 

Federal law enforcement agencies, long unable to infiltrate Nuestra Familia, began to step up their investigations in the late 1990s. In 2000 and 2001, 22 members were indicted on racketeering charges, including several who were allegedly serving as high-ranking gang leaders while confined in Pelican Bay. Thirteen of the defendants plead guilty; the other cases are still ongoing. Two of the defendants face the death penalty for ordering murders related to the drug trade. The largest of the federal investigations was Operation Black Widow. At the time of Operation Black Widow, law enforcement officials had estimated that Nuestra Familia was responsible for at least 600 murders in the previous 30 years.

In the aftermath of Operation Black Widow, the five highest ranking leaders of Nuestra Familia were transferred to a federal super maximum prison in Florence, Colorado. The written constitution of the Norteños stated that the leadership of the gang must reside in Pelican Bay State Prison in California; the relocation of the gang's leaders led to the confusion of its soldiers and a power struggle of prospective generals.

Three new generals came to power at Pelican Bay, yet two were demoted, leaving only David "DC" Cervantes as the highest ranking member of the gang in California. Cervantes' rise marked the first time in decades that the Norteños had a single leader at the helm of their criminal organization. The remaining leadership of the organization in Pelican Bay consists of Daniel "Stork" Perez, Anthony "Chuco" Guillen and George "Puppet" Franco. While all Nuestra Familia soldiers and captains in California are expected to follow the orders of Cervantes, a small percentage of the gang remains loyal to the former generals and captains imprisoned in Colorado. California Governor Arnold Schwarzenegger has complained that keeping the five remaining gang leaders located in the same prison continues to add to California gang violence, and that they should be scattered throughout different prisons. While the recognized leaders of Nuestra Familia in Pelican Bay ask that members respect the former leaders, they have been effectively stripped of their authority. The former leaders include James "Tibbs" Morado, Joseph "Pinky" Hernandez, Gerald "Cuete" Rubalcaba, Cornelio Tristan, and Tex Marin Hernandez.

While Nuestra Familia is primarily a Chicano gang, membership sometimes extends to other Latinos as well as non-Latinos. Members of the organization are considered to have taken a "blood oath" to join the gang, and are considered lifelong participants. Nuestra Familia's written constitution allegedly states that no member should prioritize women, money or drugs over their membership in the gang. Membership in the gang extends beyond prison. Women are not allowed to become full-fledged members of Nuestra Familia, but are sometimes used for communication and drug-running purposes as they are considered less likely to be noticed by law enforcement agents. The NF has a formal written constitution and claims about 2000 inmate members with an additional tens of thousands members on the outside.

Members of Nuestra Familia are known to wear red bandanas to identify themselves. Other symbols include use of the number 14, as the letter "N" is the 14th letter of the English alphabet. Nuestra Familia members often use the image of a sombrero with a dagger as their gang symbol. The primary rivals of Nuestra Familia are the Mexican Mafia. Other rivals include the Texas Syndicate, Mexikanemi, and the Aryan Brotherhood. Nuestra Familia has a loose alliance with the Black Guerrilla Family prison gang, primarily as the response of sharing similar enemies.

The Nuestra Familia/Nuestra Raza has a strong power base in Northern California because of the prison disruptive group and street gang known as the Nortenos, who identify with the Nuestra Familia and are subordinate to them. Together they are rivals of the Mexican Mafia and their affiliated Surenos, which operate out of Southern California.

In the 1970s, many Familianos migrated to Colorado, where they were later incarcerated and subsequently developed a prison gang in Colorado's prison system. Although the Colorado chapter of the NF came out of the California chapter, they have their own governing rules and leadership. As the Chicano prison population grew in the 1970s and 1980s, so too did the Familianos, and their influence within the prison subculture Northern California or the "Norte" is the original homeland of the Nuestra Familia who were called "Farmeros" in the sixties and seventies because of the large presence of farmland in Northern California. As inmates from Northern California entered the prison system, they were pulled and indoctrinated into the ways and beliefs of the NF. Thus the ideology of the "Norteno" spread.

In recent decades several regiments of Nuestra Raza and Norteno gang members have formed across cities in Northern California under the control of the Nuestra Familia. They actively participated in murder, robbery, drug trafficking, extortion, and many other crimes. Their power and influence became so prevalent the F.B.I.'s Operation Black Widow targeted these regiments for prosecution.

Nuestra Raza

La Nuestra Raza is an off-shoot of La Nuestra Familia and was formed in 1982 by the Mesa of La Nuestra Familia in response to the California Prison Administration's actions in isolating the gang in the Security Housing Unit. The NR or Northern Structure, as they were dubbed my the administration, were to represent the NF's interest and enforce their mandates on the general population yards of the prison system

NORTHERN STRUCTURE
NUESTRA FAMILIA'S JR. BRANCH

Let's talk about the gang and associate factions that I was a part of for a minute. I was an active member of La Nuestra Raza, an off-shoot and subordinate gang of La Nuestra Familia. Nuestra Familia leaders and members had been removed from the general population mainlines of California's prisons in 1980 when the first F.B.I. operation and subsequent R.I.C.O. statute sentences were handed down to the leadership. When this happened, the new leadership that arose (as one always does) decided to organize a structured division called "Nuestra Raza," more commonly known as "Northern Structure" (this is the name that CDCR Prison officials labeled the new organization with), to be there representatives and enforcers on the prison yards. The new branch was initiated in 1982 in the Administrative Segregation Units of California's Prisons and was the work of Robert "Black Bob' Vasquez, who took over the leadership of La Nuestra Familia.

This new entity would serve as a prospect base for those interested in joining Nuestra Familia, as well as to go out to the general population mainlines and recruit new Nuestra Raza members. Nuestra Raza prospects would have to earn membership into NF by following the gang's orders, and could only become a Nuestra Familia member by being pulled into the fold of the gang by a current member and under the sanction of the ruling board, called "La Mesa" (the table). La Mesa was established by "Black Bob" as an alternative to the previous regime's leadership under the authority of one leader, Supreme Nuestro General Robert "Babo" Sosa, who had been dethroned by "Black Bob", for cowardice in the face of the F.B.I. indictments for ordering a cease to the N.F.'s violence.

Gang hits were always handed down to Nuestra Raza prospects and this gave them the opportunity of proving themselves to the NF. Before a sponsored prospect can qualify as a member of the NR, he must gain knowledge of the gang's constitution officially known as the "XIV Bonds". The Nuestra Raza became the eyes, ears, and muscle of the more senior Nuestra Familia and was required to deal drugs, enforce gang rules, and fight rival prison gangs for control of yards for its father hierarchy. Nuestra Raza also sold drugs in the streets and brought in funds for ranking NF members behind bars. They operated in "Regiments" formed and commanded by an NF member.

The gang consists of united gang members recruited from violent northern California street gangs, known as Nortenos, such as San Jose, Salinas, Sacramento, Tulare County, The Central Valley, the Bay Area, and several other Northern California Cities. The Nuestra Raza is governed by the violent Nuestra Familia prison gang which controls most Northern California cities. The gang is known for committing violent crimes such as murder, home invasions and car-jacking. The Northern Structure has increased in size after the Nuestra Familia became the FBI's #1 target in 1995."

The NS is an ethnic organization with primarily Hispanic members that is sometimes known as Nuestra Raza or NR (Our Race). Its primary gang activity is narcotics trafficking. The group is antagonistic towards the Mexican Mafia and the Texas Syndicate.

NS members display many tattoos used by La Nuestra Familia. They also use XIV (fourteenth letter of the alphabet - N) to show alliance with the Norte or Norteños of Northern California. The Aztec eagle may also be seen in their drawings or tattoos.

All gangs preach loyalty, unity, carnalismo (brotherly love), etc., but will without a doubt, take you out, if you are impeding their desires and objectives or become a threat in any way. Its survival of the meanest. Personal vendettas, cronyism, favoritism, and set tripping all bring about dissention within the ranks of a gang, and sometimes . . . you lose! That's real talk. I have lived it . . . witnessed it over and over again. You can be all good within one particular set of your gang, but not very well liked by another set. I have seen gang members go from one prison where they are all good, to another prison where they get moved on (stabbed).

The larger and more powerful a gang becomes, the more diverse each faction of that gang become until they are at odds with one another. When that happens, all the politicking starts and the ground troops are the ones who pay the price, not the upper echelon. It's the way of the jungle and it ain't nothing but a gangster party! Gangsters stay loyal until they feel powerful enough to try and take over or step on another's authority. When this happens many are caught in the cross fire.

Nuestra Familia Members Battle for Control

"Robert "Black Bob" Vasquez pushes for the impeachment of Nuestra supreme commander Robert "Babo" Sosa for what he and his supporters call cowardice. Facing trial, Sosa had ordered familiano to scale back their level of violence in the face of intense federal pressure. The charges effectively create two hostile factions among familiano pitting Vasquez against Sosa for control."
http://www.gangs187.com/NFtimeline

Gangster life callin' . . . it's only a dream . . . don't bite into it . . . what you see in the movies is not the real deal . . . not even close. Most gangsters are dead or locked up, broke and strung out, or running from the police . . . not millionaires with gold tooth grilles, Rolex watches, and bling bling. They aren't rolling in Range Rovers or Escalades with their entourage, spending money hand over foot. Most gangsters I know are slammed in the S.H.U. and haven't seen daylight or had physical contact with another human besides the correctional officers that keep them. They have been in the S.H.U for years if not decades, festering and rotting away physically and mentally. They are not running around flossing and strutting their stuff with a "dime piece" (lady) on each arm. Most gangsters I know are filled with hatred, regret, and are radically violent. They are certainly not the happy go lucky, smiling, weed smoking fools you see in the various media venues. Most gangsters I know are under the watch and control of the S.H.U. Custodial Staff twenty-four/seven, not lounging in some nice club with all the amenities. So wake my young brothers! Thugging is not the life you think it is. What you see is a commodity sold on CD's or Videos with sound effects and actors. Not real bullets, real death, or real life. Real bullets kill indiscriminately and real gangsters die . . . just the way it is!

A role model in red . . .
Is not the one that you need.
Find one instead . . .
Who will teach you to read.
©©©
A gangster's the one . . .
Who will lead you astray.
He'll give you a gun . . .
And surely you'll pay.
©©©
By losing your way . . .
Or doing some time.
Instead you should pray . . .
The Lord to define.
©©©
This life of yours . . .
So you'll do the right thing.
And get what's in store . . .
From the Kingdom he brings.
©©©
It's easier to fall . . .
Prey to the game.
No need to stand tall . . .
Among seekers of fame.
©©©
But to do what is right . . .
Is much tougher, you see.
For you stand in the light . . .
To be all you can be!
©©©

Sur-13(Surenos)

Sureños are an alliance of hundreds of individual Mexican American street gangs that originated in Southern California. They are mostly found in Los Angeles and San Diego, but have spread significantly and can be found throughout much of the United States. Sureños represent themselves with symbols and phrases such as "Sur 13", "Los Sureños" and "Sureño Trece". These identifications are accompanied by the color blue, numeric code of number 13 and the Roman numeral of XIII.

"Sureños (Spanish for "Southerners") are a group of Mexican American street gangs with origins in the oldest barrios of Southern California. There are hundreds of Sureño gangs in California, and each has its own identity on the streets. Although they are based in Southern California, the influence of the Sureños has spread too many parts of the US and other countries as well. The gang's alleged roots came from a jail dispute between the Mexican Mafia (La Eme) and Nuestra Familia (NF). Those that sided with the NF aligned themselves in Northern California (norteños=northerners). Norteños appear mostly in the northern areas of California, but are also present in numbers in western states like Washington, Oregon, Colorado, and Utah. Besides Southern California, Sureños can be found in more than 20 states (primarily in southwestern, central states) and small presence in Central California, and Northern California. The largest population of Sureños can be found in Southern California, San Diego County, Orange County, Inland Empire, but specifically in Los Angeles County where 53,000 members have been documented in the city of Los Angeles alone. Norteños appear mostly in the northern areas of California, and also in southwestern and central states."

History

"The term "Sureños" meaning Southerner in Spanish. Sureño (male) Sureña (female) are the basics on what they are separated by. They originated from Southern California prison and made their way through "barrios"(hoods/neighborhoods). Throughout 1992-1993, the Mexican Mafia held meetings throughout Southern

California with local gangs to unify them as Sureños, The Mexican Mafia also taxed the local gangs and banned drive by shootings. This required the Sureños to walk up and shoot their enemies and avoid shooting non-gang members. The Sureños identify with the color blue which comes from days past when the prisons offered two standard colors of bandanas, blue and red. Their enemies are Norteños (Northerners) and have been at war since the beginning. The term was first used in the 1960s as a result of a California prison war between the Mexican Mafia (La Eme) and Nuestra Familia (NF). This war resulted in a territorial division between gang members from norteño (northern) California who aligned with NF, and those from southern California aligned with La Eme. As Eme members paroled to the streets, they were tasked with creating new cells to help facilitate more crime. In addition, paroled members explained the North versus South war occurring in prison to the young street gang members. The youngsters were told that when they did enter the prison system that they should align themselves with the other Surenos. The term Sureno was soon adopted by Hispanic street gang members throughout Southern California."

Symbols and culture

"Sureño gang members often identify themselves with the number 13; to represent the thirteenth letter of the alphabet, the letter M. This is used to pay homage to the Mexican Mafia. Surenos will use the symbols Sur, XIII, X3, 13, and 3-dots in their graffiti and tattoos. In many parts of the country they will identify themselves with the color blue, such as the Los Angeles Dodgers gear clothing and other sports teams. Mexican Mafia members may have Sureno identifiers as they were probably a Sureno gang member before being recruited into the Mexican Mafia. "http:// en.wikipedia.org

Sureno Gang Symbols

The conflict between Norteno and Sureno street gangs in California has lasted for over 30 years. The official Norte-Sur line is now roughly drawn across from Delano to Salinas with the greater Fresno area separate of both. There are few Nortenos below the line, many Surenos above it. Even this no longer holds true, as the S-N ratio is now nearly 50% in parts of Northern California. Sometimes whole gangs will move to another area because of law enforcement pressure. When a Sureno moves into a Norteno neighborhood there will be conflict! One of the largest sources of violence right now is the migration of Sureno gangs into Central and Northern California neighborhoods. Outside of California the lines are even blurrier. You can sometimes find Nortenos and Surenos living in the same vicinity where there are not well-established or traditional varrios. Sometimes you can even find Nortenos and Surenos in the same family households!"

Most California Chicano gangs claim either Norteno, Sureno (except some Maravillas), or Central Califas (F14). As gang members moved around they take this allegiance with them. Nortenos are found in most of the Western part of the United States, including Eastern Washington State and especially in Yakima County, but are not as wide spread across the entire U.S. as the Surenos are. Nortenos pride themselves in being more selective in recruitment than Surenos. Nortenos are now found as far away as Texas, Colorado, in the Mid-West, and New York where they fly under the Chicano Nation or Familia Ridas. They even have their own web sites. Many Norteno gang members will wear 49'er gear, Nebraska hats, or UNLV (Us Nortenos Love Violence). Mostly red colors called "flamed up". Make sure that this isn't the only identifier if you pull one over!

Another non-verbal identifier for the Nortenos in the past has been the Mongolian hairstyle. A top knot or ponytail growing from the top/back portion of the head. This came out of CDC and was adopted on the street. In some Northern Cal jurisdictions, law enforcement was able to educate the judges that this was another non-verbal self-admission by gang members of their Norteno affiliation/membership. Still other Nortenos will wear light blue North Carolina gear for the N.C. to signify Northern California.

We fought the Surenos throughout my whole time as a gang member. I really don't know why other than they were from down South and we were from up North. I actually knew some southerners throughout the years that I liked or could have been really good friends with had it not been for the way things were. I remember the first time I went to a California prison. I wound up in Susanville (California Correctional Center) and was way out of bounds, as the yard there was controlled by southerners. As we got off the bus, we were met by jeers and cat calls from the Surenos hanging on the fence. A few of the northerners who rode up with us locked it up (went into protective custody) immediately, but a handful of us went out to the yard.

That night after chow call and count time, I was jumped in my dormitory of 36 inmates, by two Surenos and a Border Brother, for no other reason than being from up North. The guard saw me bloody and battered and removed me out of the dorm and escorted me to the Program Lieutenant's Office for questioning. I refused to comply with the interrogation and was returned back to my dorm, where although I stayed on my toes and suited and booted, I was left alone.

We would eventually go to war with the Surenos on the yard as a matter of pride and of survival and would subsequently be transferred to other prisons. This trend continued throughout my prison stays, up until I dropped out. Once in the Transitional Housing Unit (where drop-outs are observed for up to one year prior to being released to S.N.Y), I was amazed at how we got along with one another absent all of the politics that gang involvement had thrust upon us. We had much in common and got along very well.

Gangsta life callin . . .
Bangin and ballin.
Gettin' your money . . .
And all of the honeys.
©©©
You think that it's cool . . .
Cause right now you rule.
Sitting on top . . .
Can't stop . . . won't stop!
©©©
But you better get wise . . .
To all of the lies.
Before you are through . . .
Doing the do.
©©©
Playing the role . . .
Selling your soul,
For fortune and fame . . .
Lost in the game.
©©©
It's only a dream . . .
The glory and gleam . . .
Will cause you to fall,
Lose your family and all.
©©©
Just like the rest . . .
You'll surely detest . . .
The loss of your family,
The start of insanity . . .
©©©
That will defeat . . .
And certainly deplete . . .
All that you had.
Isn't that sad?

The eventual end for an unchecked descent into the gang culture is either membership into the world of La Nuestra Familia, La Nuestra Raza, The Mexican Mafia, Aryan Brotherhood, or other prison gangs.

The other alternatives are life in prison or death! Believe it or not this is the reality. I know from personal experience. I lived it from the time of impressionable adolescence to the criminally sophisticated hard core, violent thug that I had become. It just happened. I never aspired to it. I was just kicking it with my homies and doing my thing (up to no good) throughout the years and as though it were a natural sequence of events, I had become a hard core gang member, validated by CDCR (California Department of Corrections and Rehabilitation) and locked in the S.H.U. (Security Housing Unit, Pelican Bay State Prison Supermax)

Pelican Bay State Prison Supermax Unit

©©©
What is rain?
I haven't seen it.
But I know pain . . .
I'm living it in it.
©©©
What are birds?
How would I know?
They're just words . . .
Here in this hole.
©©©
Ain't seen the sun . . .
For too many years.
But life goes on . . .
And still, no one hears,
©©©
My anguished yell . . .
From deep within.,
This concrete cell . . .
I'm dying in.
©©©
What are flowers?
I wouldn't know . . .
I see towers . . .
From within this hole.
©©©
My field of vision . . .
Is cut real short.
I've been missing . . .
On life and more.
©©©
What's the cause?
What did it cost?
You tell me . . .

Corcoran State Prison and S.H.U. Unit

Tehachapi Maximum Security State Prison and S.H.U. Unit

Control Units

Control Units are sections of a maximum or super-maximum security facility, and most fully characterize the notion of incapacitated deterrence for the most dangerous and criminally-minded offenders in the prison system. Most of the top prison gang leaders and many more of influence reside in these units. Control Units operate on a panoptical design; cells are arranged around a central security booth that lies on the ground floor. The booth's vantage point allows the constant observation of all cells at the same time through the use of security cameras and sound systems. Sometimes the security booths have computerized access to detailed case-reports of every prisoner in the unit. Prisoners are confined to their cells for 23 hours a day, and are allowed 1 hour of exercise in a tightly guarded and controlled exercise yard. Searches of inmates' cells and property are conducted on an ongoing basis in an attempt to curb communication and gang activity. However, these procedures have little or no effect on curbing gang communication.

Supermax lockups adjust to decreasing demand

Apriol 5, 2008
By Julie Carr Smyth
AP Statehouse Correspondent

"Kunta Kenyatta struggles to describe the 33 months he spent in the tight four walls of a super-maximum security cell at the Ohio State Penitentiary. "It's extreme isolation, sensory deprivation. It's hard to explain really," said Kenyatta, 39, out since 2001."

"Supermax prisons _ where inmates spend roughly 23 hours a day locked in soundproofed cells _ were trendy when Ohio cut the ribbon on its angular, steel-bedecked penitentiary April 9, 1998. A decade later, the winds favoring ultrasecure incarceration have shifted."

"Virginia and Wisconsin downgraded supermax prisons to maximum security in 2002. Virginia made the change at its notorious Wallens Ridge State Prison just four years after the facility was built. A large portion of the population of Maryland Correctional Adjustment Center, another supermax prison, was converted to less restrictive maximum security status last year. Ohio now also houses death row and lower security inmates at its penitentiary. The scenario has been repeated across the country, where early legal challenges prompted states to remove most mentally ill prisoners from supermax units and states recognized quickly that the prisons were expensive to operate and difficult to staff."

"In a nutshell, it just became clear that they were not working," said David Fathi, director of U.S. programs at Human Rights Watch. "They were more trouble and expense than they were worth." Supermax prisons were built to house inmates convicted of serious crimes who caused trouble in prison, including gang activity, subversive behavior or violence against staff. Ohio's went up after the deadly 1993 Lucasville prison uprising."

"Dave Johnson, the penitentiary's first warden, recalls a kind of super-maximum space race among state corrections departments at the time, each wanting their facility to be the first, the biggest or the best. The first inmates arrived at Ohio's prison in May 1998. "I got a call one morning and the man on the other end said, 'I don't know you but I already hate you,'" Johnson recalled. "It was the warden from the Illinois Supermax, and we had gotten our accreditation before he did." Johnson said the Supermax was viewed as much safer than the Lucasville prison."

"Philosophically, the big thing that we wanted to avoid was an atmosphere of retaliation, where inmates would do something, staff would retaliate, then inmates would retaliate, then things would spiral downhill," he said. "It started out right away (at the Supermax) where staff would be safe, so they wouldn't be fearful of inmates, wouldn't dread coming to work, and it was a very positive, upbeat environment."

"In Maryland, prisons had also become deadly, said Mark Vernarelli, a spokesman for the state Department of Public Safety and Correctional Services. Its Supermax was built in the wake of two prison guard murders, one in a prison a touring judge labeled "the innermost circle of hell.""

"At the peak of the supermax craze in 2000, more than 30 states were operating one or more supermax prisons, holding an estimated 20,000 prisoners, according to a National Institute of Corrections study and research by Human Rights Watch. By 2006, the number of prisoners held in supermax custody had fallen to 2,378 in 10 states, according to statistics from the American Correctional Association. Ohio's Supermax provides a prime example. Only 53 of 553 inmates are held in the extreme isolation."

"The cell of a supermax inmate measures 89.7 square feet, enough room for a ledge for his cot, a small desk and stool, a set of three small bookshelves (one used for the TV), and a toilet and sink. Inmates are allotted a 15-minute shower and one hour for exercise each weekday. Meals and most routine medical care take place in the cell. All visits with outsiders are non-contact."

"On a recent day, some inmates released for their hour reprieve from isolation were dashing end-to-end in a cellblock, some were doing vigorous pull-ups, push-ups and knee bends, while others were just talking. "Just to endure the conditions takes a very strong person or else a person who can retreat into a very narrow place," said Alice Lynd, part of a husband-wife attorney team from Niles that has fought Ohio's Supermax in court. "You lose any interest in staying alive. There's no ability to concentrate, you don't get normal feedback." With the prisons' popularity waning, states also found that there were not enough ultra-bad inmates to justify all the glistening new ultra-high security cells _ conceived, Fathi says, "not by corrections professionals, but by politicians trying to look tougher on crime than the next person."

"Walter Dickey, a former Wisconsin prisons chief who served as court monitor in a challenge to the state's former Supermax,

the Wisconsin Secure Program Facility, said the excess capacity remains a problem. "Because there's a bed shortage overall in most prison systems, there's pressure to use supermax beds because they're the only empty beds in the systems," said Dickey, now a professor at the University of Wisconsin Law School. "That was an issue with our state's Supermax, and one that most corrections departments need to look in the eye. And it's not easy to look it in the eye because it's not easy to know what to do."

"Virginia's Wallens Ridge is now nearly full _ housing 1,150 maximum-security inmates in 1,200 available beds. By contrast, 795 of the 1,200 beds available at the state's remaining Supermax, Red Onion, are in use, said Virginia Department of Corrections spokesman Larry Traylor. Corrections professionals were also divided over how extensively to use supermax, something that state law generally leaves up to their discretion. Ohio's penitentiary created two tiers of security for its supermax inmates after the Lynds' litigation had begun _ allowing the better behaved ones slightly more mobility and more access to perks such as library books and commissary items. "I look at 10 years ago and we had one purpose: to protect and serve, to take the worst of the worst," said Marcus Hill, a member of the prison's program staff. "Now you can tell how far we've come. We ask the inmate, 'What are your needs?' Before, we gave them their needs."

"Kenyatta, sentenced to 30 years for robbery and attempted murder, said the "worst of the worst" label stings. "They say these are the worst people, that they couldn't get along in society," said Kenyatta, who now chairs the prisoner advocacy group CURE-Ohio. "Well, I'm out here in society and I'm very successful. I have my own business, a lot of charitable causes and everything." Despite the prisons' evolution, Dickey doesn't believe the Supermax will disappear. "We wanted to make them as good as we could. There were some people who wanted to make them as bad as possible in hopes they would be shut down," he said. "But I think there's the potential now to have the best of both worlds, to have those who straight out do bad things be segregated but not to have it be so onerous on the people who are in there."
http://www.ohio.com/news

©©©
Gnashing of teeth . . .
And piercing screams.
Nightmares defeat . . .
All of your dreams.
©©©
Souls, tortured and raw . . .
Buried here deep.
Forget what you saw . . .
Or you won't sleep.
©©©
Minds eroding away . . .
All over the place.
Making their way . . .
In a drug induced haze.
©©©
That's how some cope . . .
Inside the S.H.U.
All full of dope . . .
Just to get through.
©©©
Others act out . . .
In violence and pain.
They scream and they shout . . .
Just to stay sane.
©©©
This is the S.H.U.!
I thought that you knew!

The only reward I received from this was to spend over twenty years behind bars, in one prison or another, in more than one state, and most of it in Administrative Segregation. I carry the physical scars of gang warfare (I have been stabbed by rival gang members), and the emotional scars of things I have seen or experienced. I carry them every single day of my life. I am reminded of the ugly truth of who I had become every time I shave or look in the mirror. But I would not want to have that scar on my face removed, because it is a daily reminder of who I was and who I don't want to be. It now keeps me in check.

But even with that said, I am one of the lucky ones (if you could call it that) because I am still living and I am free from prison, and free from the madness. I am still healthy, and not too old. Many of my ex-homies have perished in one way or another, relative to their involvement in the gang lifestyle. Many have been given life sentences or sit on death row. Many of them are no longer with us, having died because of gang warfare or inter gang politics. They have been riddled with bullets, viciously stabbed, shot by prison guards or police, and much more. Most have also done this to others, as have I. The bottom line and finality is that because of their choices, they are dead or in prison. There lives a terrible waste due to gang violence. The game is definitely not about it . . . not by a long shot . . . and with this book I hope to emphasize that.

It's end of the road . . . end of the line . . . doing life in the S.H.U. In an 8'X10' concrete cell with a concrete bed, twenty-three hours a day. Yeah . . . now you're a big shot . . . the big homie . . . shot caller . . . wow! Now what! Where do you go from there? Nowhere . . . because you're stuck in that cage like a wild animal. What can you do? Not much. Go to the yard every other day? A concrete or caged-in square yard about twice the size of your cell? Now you're doing big things! Take a shower? Only when your keepers allow you to!

Sure you got money . . . you're a baller . . . but what does that get you. You can only spend $55.00 per month and everything you buy goes stale before you can eat it all (no plastic or containers are allowed in the S.H.U. because gang members have used these items in the past to manufacture weapons to assault one another or to assault staff members). Sure, you have power and can have someone whacked (killed) at your whim. But you cannot take a walk when you feel up to it . . . smell fresh flowers . . . enjoy the sights and sounds of the birds in the sky . . . or hear the laughter of an innocent child. Sure you are physically fit and mentally sharp (an exercise regimen and self-education are required activities by most gangs) . . . but what does that get you? It doesn't get you out of your cell. You can't compete in sports, go for a swim, or participate in a college debate, because your bad ass can't have contact with anyone else. For all the power and awe you hold, you are simply a caged criminal at the control of your state sanctioned captors. That's not a very good trade off. It's over . . . you're done . . . there is no turning back.

©©©
This gangster life . . .
Is not the way.
It's not a game . . .
You want to play.
©©©
If you think . . .
There's honor here,
Let me tell you . . .
There's only hate and fear.
©©©
Mistrust . . .
Within the ranks.
On this reality . . .
You can bank.
©©©
No one cares . . .
Who you are,
Because they are all . . .
Trying to be the star!
©©©
They'll trample you . . .
Without a doubt.
To get ahead . . .
They'll take you out!
©©©
Just the way it is . . .
My friend.
But you'll find out . . .
In the end.
©©©

Solitary confinement is a special form of imprisonment in which a prisoner is denied or is given only limited contact with any other persons, though often with the exception of members of prison staff. It is sometimes employed as a form of punishment beyond incarceration for a prisoner, and has been cited as an additional measure of protection from the criminal or is given for violations of prison regulations.

It is also used as a form of protective custody and to implement a suicide watch. It is considered by many legal scholars to be a form of psychological torture when the period of confinement is longer than a few weeks or is continued indefinitely. Solitary confinement is colloquially referred to in American English as the 'hotbox', the 'hole', 'lockdown', the 'SHU' (pronounced 'shoe') - an acronym for security housing unit, or the 'pound'; and in British English as the 'block' or the 'cooler'. Those who accept the practice consider it necessary for prisoners who are considered dangerous to other people ("the most predatory" prisoners), those who might be capable of leading crime groups even from within, or those who are kept 'incommunicado' for purported reasons of national security. Finally, it may be used for prisoners who are at high risk of being attacked by other inmates, such as pedophiles, celebrities, or witnesses who are in prison themselves. This latter form of solitary confinement is sometimes referred to as protective custody.

©©©
Voyages unfinished . . .
Time travels on.
Some things diminished . . .
Others long gone.
©©©
Hopes put asunder . . .
Dreams dashed away.
Oh what a blunder . . .
I made that day.
©©©
Took a man's life . . .
Not even a care.
I used a knife . . .
Now I'm sitting here.
©©©
End of the line . . .
For hurting another.
Doing my time . . .
Gave pain to his mother.

©©©
Can't shed a tear . . .
I'm already lost.
Tremble in fear . . .
Look at the cost.
©©©
Don't replicate . . .
Things I have done.
Don't live in hate . . .
It's the same song.
©©©
Just look at me . . .
No longer free!

CHAPTER SEVEN

Other street gangs

"In 2004, the FBI created the MS-13 National Gang Task Force to combat gang activity in the United States. A year later, the FBI helped create National Gang Intelligence Center."

"In the United States in 2006 there were approximately 785,000 active street gang members, according to the National Youth Gang Center."

"Los Angeles County is considered the <u>Gang Capital of America</u>, with an estimated 120,000 (41,000 in the City) gang members although Chicago actually has a higher rate of gang membership per capita than Los Angeles. Also, the state of Illinois has a higher rate of gang membership (8-11 gang members per 1,000 populations) than California (5-7 gang members per 1,000 populations). There were at least 30,000 gangs and 800,000 gang members active across the USA in 2007. About 900,000 gang members lived "within local communities across the country," and about 147,000 were in U.S. prisons or jails in 2009. By 1999, Hispanics accounted for 47% of all gang members, Blacks 31%, Whites 13%, and Asians 6%."

"Tribal leaders say Native American communities are being overwhelmed by gang violence and drug trafficking. A Dec. 13, 2009 New York Times article about growing gang violence on the Pine Ridge Indian Reservation estimated that there were 39 gangs

with 5,000 members on that reservation alone. Navajo country recently reported 225 gangs in its territory. There are between 25,000 and 50,000 gang members in Central America's El Salvador. The Mexican drug cartels have as many as 100,000 foot soldiers. More than 1,000 gangs were known to be operating in the UK in 2009."

"The FBI estimates the size of the four Italian organized crime groups to be approximately 25,000 members and 250,000 affiliates worldwide. The Russian, Chechen, Ukrainian, Georgian, Armenian, and other former Soviet organized crime groups or "Bratvas" have approximately 300,000 people affiliated with them. The Yakuza are among one of the largest crime organizations in the world. In Japan, as of 2005, there are some 102,400 known members. Hong Kong's Triads include up to 160,000 members in the 21st century. It was estimated that in the 1950s, there were 300,000 Triad members in Hong Kong."

"There were at least 30,000 gangs and 800,000 gang members active across the USA in 2007,] up from 731,500 in 2002 and 750,000 in 2004."
From Wikipedia, the free encyclopedia

Read the following current article about a gang who has infiltrated and terrorized a community, and how even though this has happened many witnesses denied the very existence of the gang. This gang has strong ties to the Nuestra Familia and Nuestra Raza prison gangs.

Yolo County Judge Issues Gang Injunction
Posted Date: 6/20/2011 9:30 AM

<u>*Press Release*</u>

After a 54 day trial with testimony from over 286 witnesses and over 800 exhibits, Yolo County Judge finds by clear and convincing evidence that the Broderick Boys is a criminal street gang that has created a public nuisance in the City of West Sacramento.

(Woodland, CA) - Yolo County District Attorney Jeff Reisig announced that on June 16, 2011, Yolo County Superior Court Judge Kathleen White issued a final "Judgment Granting Injunction After Trial" against the Broderick Boys criminal street gang in West Sacramento. The gang injunction issued by the court imposes a curfew and restricts other activities of gang members in a defined area within West Sacramento called the "Safety Zone."

The trial in the case started on July 12, 2010, and concluded on December 15, 2010. The parties were permitted to submit post-trial briefing statements. The evidence during the 54 day trial included over 286 witnesses, a viewing of the Safety Zone in West Sacramento by the judge, and over 800 exhibits.

After hearing all of evidence at trial and reviewing the exhibits and the post-trial briefs, Judge White found that the Broderick Boys is a criminal street gang, the Broderick Boys has created a public nuisance in the Safety Zone by its conduct and activities, and the public nuisance caused by the Broderick Boys has created irreparable harm to those who live and work in the Safety Zone.

In her written decision after the court trial, Judge White stated, "The court found the testimony of the victims and percipient witnesses to the crimes described during the trial particularly credible and compelling...." Additionally, Judge White "found credible the law enforcement officers who testified about their response to the crimes in the Safety Zone...." Discussing the defense witnesses, Judge White found them equally credible in their description of the Safety Zone as a community with strong family ties." However, "the court found less credible the testimony of these defense witnesses as to the nonexistence of the Broderick Boys gang. These reasons included the witnesses' relationships to named defendants and their apparent motive to minimize the defendants' actions, their lack of personal knowledge regarding certain events, their use of the phrase 'I don't recall,' and/or gaps in their knowledge or recollection." Judge White concluded, "Of particular note in the court's deliberations: much of the evidence presented by the plaintiff [District Attorney's Office] was uncontroverted, and much of the argument in the defendants' closing briefs assumed facts not supported by the evidence at trial."

Judge White also ruled that her order granting the injunction will expire after seven years, finding that during this time frame law enforcement should be able to use the injunction to reduce the gang activity so that the injunction is no longer necessary.

Yolo County Press Release

Unfortunately, although these gang injunctions are the order of the day, they do very little to impact or curtail the activities of their intended targets. These gangs simply choose to ignore these injunctions and continue their activity until they are caught and sent to prison, since violations of the imposed gang injunctions do not levy very much time behind bars. And besides, going back to prison for a short time is like going to a reunion, for most gang members. We used to call it, "getting a tune up", because you are going to eat healthy and work out doing "la maquina" (the machine, an exercise regimen that is mandatory for all northern Hispanics).

Say, lil thug . . .
Let me holla . . .
Stop all that flossing . . .
And popping your collar.
©©©
Give me a minute . . .
To tell you what's real . . .
About what happens . . .
When you bang and you steal.
©©©
You wind up in prison . . .
Locked in a cell . . .
Only a short step . . .
From the fires of hell.
©©©

Think you're a tough guy?
Wait till you're there . . .
Brutal reality . . .
Is yours if you dare.
©©©
Just bring it . . .
Silly young fool . . .
But be ready . . .
To follow the rules.
©©©
You heard me . . .
That's what I said . . .
Just break one . . .
And surely you're dead.
©©©
Convicts and gangsters . . .
They're who run this . . .
Just act up . . .
And you'll be dismissed.
©©©
Not stuck in the corner . . .
Like you were in school . . .
But stuck in the chest . . .
You silly young fool!

Gangs continue to threaten our lives, our homes, or property, and our personal security. If left unchecked they can and will threaten our very existence. Every minute of every day someone in America is unduly affected in one way or another by the blight of gangs. They are a scourge on our society and a viable threat to our safety and well-being. We cannot, as individuals and on a personal level, ignore the fact that they do exist, and that they wreak havoc, anguish, and frustration on us as they continue to thrive.

In 2005, a spokeswoman for the California Department of Corrections and Rehabilitation said there are over 160,000 inmates in California prisons. Estimates put the prison gang population at 803 members, 900 associates, 325 inactive members and 1,050 dropouts. That is 2028 hardcore prison gang members in a prison population of about 160,000 inmates or roughly about 1.2% of the population. Yet this small percentage of inmates control the prison yards of California as well as various neighborhoods, towns, and cities. If that is not a testament to their power and influence, I don't know what is. And I'm not even taking into account those who dropped out.

The following is an example of the proliferation of gangs just within the greater Los Angeles area. Please keep in mind that this is only concerning the Crips gang. You still have to take into account the neighborhood Sureno gangs, the Mexican Mafia, the Bloods, the Nazi Lowriders, and other various gangs that thrive within this geographical locale. The number of Surenos in Los Angeles outnumbers Crips and Bloods combined.

Cities and places in Los Angeles County Where Crip Gangs Flourish

Altadena	[1 gang]	Inglewood	[1 gang]	Paramount	[1 gang]
Athens	[15 gangs]	Lakewood	[0 gangs]	Pasadena	[1 gang]
Carson	[6 gangs]	Lancaster	[3 gangs]	Pomona	[6 gangs]
Compton	[22 gangs]	Long beach	[22 gangs]	Rosewood	[1 gang]
Duarte	[1 gang]	Los Angeles	[93 gangs]	Santa Monica	[1 gang]
Florence	[5 gangs]	Lynwood	[1 gang]	Torrance	[1 gang]
Gardena	[5 gangs]	Hawthorne	[2 gangs]	W. Covina	[5 gangs]

Crips are just one distinct group of gang-members. You can see how gangs proliferate. It is an epidemic and it is pandemic and education is the only way to deal with it. Too many young people walk blindly into gang membership with little or no knowledge of its dangers. We try to screen ourselves off from this problem by feigning ignorance or pretending it doesn't exist, or that it doesn't affect us. But the bold truth is that it's right there in our faces and it exists on a level such as never before. We have to meet it head on, understand what makes it work, and deal with it on that level. All of us!

Below is a list of prison gang profiles, including location of operation, formation year, objectives, structure, organization, and known-leaders, for your information and to help enlighten you. The problem is of massive proportions. These are just some of the more prominent and violent gangs that exist. There are so many more that aren't mentioned here that it simply astounds the mind.

Bloods

The Bloods are a street gang founded in Los Angeles, California. The gang is widely known for its rivalry with the Crips. They are identified by the red color worn by their members. However because of the efforts of Stanley "Tookie" Williams have pretty much resolved their issues with the Crips.

Border Brothers

The Border Brothers gang was founded in 1989 by Sergio Gonzalez-Martinez and other street thugs in Tijuana, Mexico. The Mexican gang spread into California in 1990 and began recruiting criminal illegal immigrants in barrios across San Diego, Los Angeles, Fresno and Oakland.

Crips

The Crips started as a street gang in Los Angeles when Raymond Washington and Stanley Tookie Williams set up the gang in 1969 in East LA. Stanley Tookie Williams was co-founder of the Crips when he was only 17 years old, and given the death penalty in San Quentin State Prison on December 13, 2005. Raymond Washington, co- founder, was murdered in 1979.

Dixie Mafia

The Dixie Mafia is a criminal organization based in Biloxi, Mississippi, and operated primarily in the Southern United States, in the 1970s. The group uses each member's talents in various crime categories to help move stolen merchandise, illegal alcohol, and illegal drugs. It is also particularly well-known for violence.

KUMI 415

Was formed in Folsom State Prison. Along with the Crips and the Bloods, 415 KUMI Nation members have recently provided recruitment pools for the Black Guerilla Family (BGF), a gang with similarly large numbers in the Bay area and Northern California. In the Monterey County Jail, brief alliances have been reported among the Bloods, Crips, and KUMI 415 during period leading up to Stanley Tookie Williams' execution. KUMI is the Swahili word for the number 10, and the sum of 415 is 10. 415 also refers to San Francisco's area code.

MS-13

Mara Salvatrucha (commonly abbreviated as MS, Mara, and MS-13) is a transnational criminal gang that originated in Los Angeles and has spread to other parts of the United States, Canada, Mexico, and Central America. The majority of the gang is ethnically composed of Central Americans and active in urban and suburban areas.

Trinitarios

The Trinitarios AKA 3NI are a violent New York-based multinational organization composed of Latinos.[1] Trinitario was established in 1989 within the New York state prison system[2] and since spilled into the streets, with chapters in all five boroughs of New York City.

Outlaw Motorcycle gangs

We did things for one another in furtherance of our mutual agenda. That is the business of making money and unadulterated criminality. I would take some of my homies with me and do some collection or enforcement actions for my biker associates, or they would do likewise for us. We hung out, did dope, made money, and engaged in all sorts of sexual debauchery. It was just the way of the world in which I lived and I was good at living in that world. I didn't care and it didn't matter. All that mattered was that I was a top dog in a dog eat dog world. I always got one of the biggest bones and ran things my way. Sure, I was under the rule of the gang, but I had quite a bit of leeway as long as I produced.

The outlaw motorcycle gangs have been around for many years, since the nineteen-forties. They distribute narcotics, sell firearms, steal vehicles (especially motorcycles), and are involved in all sorts of violent crimes. There are several of these gangs across the Ameerican frontier. Their origin is rooted in the philosophy of always having a good time and doing whatever they wanted with little or no regard for the law. These clubs flourished in the nineteen-sixties amid the widespread use of illegal drugs and the rebel era. Motorcycle gangs took advantage of this and began to manufacture and distribute methamphetamines as a way of funding themselves.

These gangs are made up of chapters and a mother club who directs the different chapters. Each of the chapters will have a representative from the mother club who has direct supervision over the chapter. Chapter presidents fall under the control of these advisors. The mother club establishes and enforces policy for the organization and has final authority over club matters.

They poison our streets with drugs, violence, and all manner of crime.

Some 20,000 violent street gangs, motorcycle gangs, and prison gangs with nearly one million members are criminally active in the U.S. today. Many are sophisticated and well organized; all use violence to control neighborhoods and boost their illegal money-making activities, which include robbery, drug and gun trafficking, fraud, extortion, and prostitution rings. We're redoubling our

efforts to disrupt and dismantle gangs through intelligence-driven investigations and new initiatives and partnerships.
http://www.fbi.gov/about-us/investigate/vc_majorthefts/gangs/gangs

This is just a small number of significant gangs across the United States. Believe me when I tell you that there are many more. I just wanted to give you an idea as to the prevalence of major, highly criminally sophisticated gangs within our society. I would venture to say that you could probably multiply the number of gangs listed above by several hundred and still be short.

During the last two twenty-two years or so, the United States has seen the youth gang problem grow at an alarming rate. According to the National Youth Gang Center, the number of cities with youth gang problems has increased from an estimated 286 with more than 2,000 gangs and nearly 100,000 gang members in 1980 to about 2,000 cities with more than 25,000 gangs and 650,000 members in 1995. The growth is astounding and it continues to climb ever higher. Youth gangs are present and active in nearly every state, as well as in Puerto Rico and other territories. Few large cities are gang-free and even many cities and towns with populations of less than 25,000 are reporting gang problems. Thus, the issue of youth gangs is now affecting new localities, such as small towns and rural areas.

© © ©
Say li'l bro . . .
I bet you didn't know . . .
That I used to be you.
It's sad, but it's true.
© © ©
I did all the things . . .
That brought me the bling.
Brought me the fame . . .
All up in this game.
© © ©
But now li'l bro . . .
I'm stuck in this hole,
Never to see . . .
Another day free.

©©©
I thought I was hard . . .
Held high regard,
For my rag and my crew.
Just like you do.
©©©
Listen li'l bro . . .
I want you to know . . .
This life ain't about it.
The prisons are crowded . . .
©©©
With convicts like me,
Who wanted to be . . .
Up in the mix,
Putting down licks.
©©©
I wish li'l bro . . .
That you would just go,
In a different direction . . .
Make a selection,
©©©
That's better than mine.
Make your life shine.
Please li'l bro . . .

Gang members represent serious concerns to juvenile correctional facilities, particularly in the areas of safety and security. Juvenile correctional management and staff must cope with developing suppression strategies for gang behavior and activity within their facilities. Likewise, juvenile corrections professionals who work in institutions or facilities housing gang-involved youths must pro-actively develop and refine programs that address gang involvement as a treatment issue and tailor treatment to get through the mind-set and defenses of urbanized, hard-core, streetwise youths.

Otherwise, we will have perpetual aimlessness and recidivism among the gang-affiliated population. It becomes a vicious circle with new juveniles recruited and enlightened every single day. Understand that the gangster lifestyle is thrown at our children from all angles, in every part of their young lives. It is an oncoming and raging storm, and if we don't arm our children with the proper tools, it will engulf them. It comes to them in song, in movies, in television, and in the social media. Gangs even have web-sites! Can you believe that? That is how permissive of a society we live in. Gangs should not be allowed to advertise themselves on the internet. That's simply outrageous.

The gang culture comes to them in dress styles, in school, and various other avenues. Fighting back with family values, good morals, proper education, and alternative activities such as sports, will help to combat the onslaught. Everyone needs to belong . . . to feel connected with others and be with others who share attitudes, interests, and circumstances that resemble their own. People choose friends who accept and like them and see them in a favorable light.

Our children are being drawn into the growing sphere of influence brought on by the gang culture. They have no knowledge about the dark side of gang involvement. They don't see the brutal murders and the lack of integrity. They don't see the total brutality of the lifestyle. They only see the money, the girls, and the glamour. It is our responsibility to enlighten them and open the doors for other more productive alternatives before they get lost in the lust of gangs, for once lost, their involvement becomes an ever gradual descent into the depths of violence, greed, hatred, mayhem, and murder until they become firmly entrenched in the lifestyle. They become criminally sophisticated, violent, and filled with contempt for social structure.

Today's laws take the power away from parents with regard to discipline. Their now exists a very fine line between discipline and child abuse in our society, and parents are reluctant to provide the necessary discipline that their children need. Since they are hesitant to test the waters, children run rampant over them. Even the bible counsels us not to spare the rod. Family has been diminished to a bunch of related people living together under the same roof, and simply tolerating one another. There is no unity, barely any love, and certainly no communication.

The family fabric has been rent and respect is lacking. It has been torn asunder by a multitude of malevolent and malignant factors. Some are manifestations of social disorder and yet others are of a personal nature. Ultimately the underlying issue is that we, as a family unit have lost touch with what is and is not important in the development of deep-seated morality. Have said that, I believe that our short-comings, society wide, create a vacuum where are children, who are our future, are left to their own machinations without guidance, and are being defined by our permissiveness and lack of concern.

Youngster gone mad . . .
It's really quite sad.
Doing this and doing that . . .
Strapped up with a gat.
©©©
Won't be a minute . . .
Before he's deep up in it.
Did something rash . . .
Trying to make some cash.
©©©
Hanging with the crowd . . .
Bangin' and being loud.
Lost in a world of drugs . . .
Him and his fellow thugs.
©©©
Running here, running there . . .
Not even trying to care.
Daring one another on . . .
Motivated by a rap song.
©©©
It's the life that they live . . .
Something's gotta give.
Trying to idolize . . .
The thugs they glamorize.
©©©
Sending out the message . . .
Of hatred and of rage.
Can't we stop this madness?
That fills our lives with sadness!
©©©

We need to fight back and take our streets back and instill the family values that we experienced in years gone by. We need social reform, not from the politicians, who have no integrity and change with the blowing of the winds of public opinion and the voter approval polls, adapting to the mood of the moment and who have even less integrity than criminals do. But that is my opinion.

No this needs to be accomplished on a personal level, family by family, block by block, neighborhood by neighborhood . . . and so on. We need to stop what we are doing . . . take a look around us at the roiling chaos . . . and listen to the anguished outbursts of our youth.

©©©
Incorrigible youths . . .
Way out of line,
Our battle to lose . . .
If we don't define . . .
©©©
A well thought out plan,
To bring them all back . . .
From where they ran,
Because of our slack.
©©©
In the company of . . .
Gangs, drugs, and violence . . .
Enough is enough!
Let's not be silent . . .
©©©
Not anymore!
It'll only get worse . . .
That's what's in store,
If we don't disperse . . .
©©©
The gangs and the cliques . . .
That have formed,
From all of our kids,
A huge rising storm.
©©©
Unless you stand up . . .
And fight readily,
It surely won't stop . . .
All of us lose,
So there's no excuse.

Here are a few gang-prevention strategies:

- *The family and the community are essential to the development of the child's social, emotional, and physical needs. If the family is the source of love, guidance, and protection that youths seek, they are not forced to search for these basic needs from a gang. The family and community share responsibility for teaching children the risk of drugs.*
- *Strong education and training are directly related to a youth's positive development. Young people who successfully participate in and complete education have greater opportunities to develop into reasonable adults.*
- *Graffiti removal reduces the chance that crimes will be committed. Since gangs use graffiti to mark their turf, advertise themselves, and claim credit for a crime, quick removal is essential.*
- *Conflict resolution programs teach gangs how to deal better with conflicts and help eliminate gang intimidation tactics.*
- *Recreational programs such as sports, music, drama, and community activities help build a sense of self-worth and self-respect in young people. Youth involved in such activities are less likely to seek membership in a gang.*

From Research Review: Gang Violence and Prevention by Mary H. Lees, M.A., Human Development Department; Mary Deen, M.A., Extension Youth Development Specialist; and Louise Parker, Ph.D., Extension Family Economics Specialist; Washington State University

Some of the reasons for joining a gang may include:

- *A search for love, structure, and discipline*
- *A sense of belonging and commitment*
- *The need for recognition and power*
- *Companionship, training, excitement, and activities*
- *A sense of self-worth and status*

- *A place of acceptance*
- *The need for physical safety and protection*
- *A family tradition*

"Risk Factors for Joining a Gang

- *Racism: When young people encounter both personal and institutional racism (i.e., systematic denial of privileges), the risks are increased. When groups of people are denied access to power, privileges, and resources, they will often form their own anti-establishment group.*
- *Poverty: A sense of hopelessness can result from being unable to purchase wanted goods and services. Young people living in poverty may find it difficult to meet basic physical and psychological needs which can lead to a lack of self-worth and pride. One way to earn cash is to join a gang involved in the drug trade.*
- *Lack of a support network: Gang members often come from homes where they feel alienated or neglected. They may turn to gangs when their needs for love are not being met at home. Risks increase when the community fails to provide sufficient youth programs or alternatives to violence.*
- *Media influences: Television, movies, radio, and music all have profound effects on youth development. Before youth have established their own value systems and are able to make moral judgments, the media promotes drugs, sex, and violence as an acceptable lifestyle."*

Protective Factors

- *Well-developed social and interpersonal skills*
- *High sense of self-esteem, self-efficacy, and personal responsibility*
- *Reflectivity, rather than impulsive thought and behavior*
- *Internal locus of control (i.e., the belief of being able to influence environment in a positive manner)*

- *Flexible coping strategies, well-developed problem-solving skills and intellectual abilities*

http://www.focusas.com/Gangs

What factors influence a person's decision to join a gang?

Man Charged With Fatally Shooting Young Mother, Injuring Her Brother
"Chicago police charged Reuben Navarro of murdering an 18 year old mother and injuring her little brother on April 26th, 2009. He fired on a car with the victims in it. This Chicago evening was tragic. A young mother was fatally shot, and a young boy was severely injured. The boy said he was so scared he was moving to a new town."

"The boy didn't press charges on the killer because he was afraid that he was going to send his men after him. The boy was previously in a gang. The mother, Jennifer Figueroa, was visiting her grandma according to her boyfriend. The boyfriend said he was sitting watching the baby, when a man came out of an alley shooting his gun and saying something. According to the boyfriend the killer shot the wrong people.

This article seems like another sad gang story. It was stupid for the man to kill the innocent people. This is what happens when you get wrapped up in gangs. The killer was dumb for shooting the wrong people, and even dumber for wanting to shoot someone. Areas in big cities like Detroit, Chicago, and L.A. should prevent these crimes because these are the areas were gang violence is occurring. Plus, the boy dropped charges because he feared the man was going to send men after him. That is how I feel about this article.'

Gang-Risk Children "Should Be In Care"
'British police say that children who have older brothers or sisters that are in a gang are at higher risk to join a gang. There has been a sudden increase of young teenagers joining gangs, usually influenced by older brothers or sisters that are in gangs. The most recent gang related death was a 12 year old boy. "Gangs are a quick way to screw up your life," said an officer.'

'People who have an influence of gangs in from their neighborhood, house, friends, relatives, and even city need more help than other children. Police say there are 171 street gangs just in London. Michael Todd explained this to teens at a gang prevention summit, led by the Prime Minister of the U.K. Sir Ian thinks that peer pressure is the number one key of gang recruitment. A spokesman said, "Getting involved with gangs can be a short cut to serious violence in which young people are the most likely victims."

I agree with this article saying that people who have an influence from older siblings to join a gang need special help. It is true because a person usually does what their older sibling does to be cool or fit in. In this article, children joining gangs isn't a problem just in the U.S., it is all over the world. I agree that gangs are a quick way to screw up your life. It is true that young gangsters are usually the targets.

Who's at Risk of Joining a Gang?

'Any person can join a gang. A boy or girl, rich or poor, dumb or smart, any family, and any race can join a gang. Males, drugs, has a family member in a gang, people who live with one parent, people who are poor, people who are bad in school, and people who have been neglected are all characteristics of gang members. Life is tough for these people. They go to gangs to escape problems, but get there self in more. Some people join gangs to be cool.'

'These characteristics don't guarantee that the person will join a gang. Identifying these characteristics can help a community find and help these children. Gang membership can start at an early age. That is why we need to get the message out to people at an early age so it can stick with them for a long time. A child in a gang can affect the whole family.'

'I believe it is exactly true that those characteristics are a big influence on a child to join a gang. It is also true that anyone can be in a gang just like the Socs in the book because they are smart, wealthy, and have good parents and are gang members. People do join gangs to be cool, or from peer pressure. We do need to get the message of not joining gangs to people when they are little so it can stick with them when they are older. That's is what I think about this article.'

Works Cited
Parenting Teens. 1997. Project Safe Neighborhood. 6 July. 2007
<http://parentingteens.about.com/cs/gangviolence/a/gangs2.htm >

Steele, John. "Gang-risk children "should be in care"." Telegraph. 4 May. 2007.
Sweeney, Anne. "Man charged with fatally shooting young mother, injuring her brother
In Logan Square." Chicago Sun-Times. 28 April. 2009

CHAPTER EIGHT

My qualifications

As we discuss all aspects of this unfortunate phenomenon, it is my hope to awaken the sleeping giant of American morality and to motivate individuals into some sort of action, a positive action toward healthier morals and stricter standards. That is the only way to combat this issue. Hit them at the recruitment level by arming our youth with education and integrity to resist the pull of gangs. You can't fight them on their terms. Look at the law enforcement. They try to do so and these thugs take it to law enforcement with all levels of violence. Enacting new laws doesn't do anything to curb the trend. Building more prisons has not been the answer as they have become colleges of criminal sophistication for a much younger and more dangerous type of gang member. We need to hit them at their recruitment levels in order to stop them.

This action is dependent upon each individual's capabilities. We can't wait around for someone else to carry the ball. We can't wait around for politicians to find the answer. The answer is right in front of us, but we must all be willing to do our part to bring morality and enlightenment to the forefront. We must enlighten our youth and provide some sort of direction in their lives. It must first start in our homes and our communities, and then the much broader spectrum of our society.

But before I go any further, allow me to qualify myself to even speak on this subject. I don't speak from an academic point of view, although I have done much research on the subject to broaden and enhance my scope of understanding from both sides of the equation, but more importantly, I speak from an insider's point of view, as one who has been in the so-called trenches of the gang lifestyle. Of one who has lived the life for most of three decades, and one who has experienced the madness first-hand. Of one who has been at both ends of a prison manufactured weapon.

I'm not trying to be your friend . . .
Or impress you with my words.
I only ask for you to give me ten . . .
To put you up on something you haven't heard.
©©©
The game is talked about hella swell . . .
It's given fame, prestige, and even class.
But no one tells you about the time they fell . . .
When the game left them flattened on their ass!
©©©
Very few survive it to the very end . . .
And even less stay on top for very long.
Most will find themselves beginning to descend . . .
To the pits of hell with others who were wrong!
©©©
Survival of the meanest is what it's all about . . .
With a measure of lies and deceit thrown right in.
And no matter how much you scream and shout . . .
To lie, and cheat, and kill is the only way to win.
©©©
The homies who swore to have your back . . .
Will be the first to stomp all over you.
Because in this game the cards are stacked . . .
And most players haven't got a clue.
©©©
You'll be good one day . . . and be all bad the next . . .
Or have to move on the guy you grew up with.
For in this game all the rules are mixed . . .
And keep changing with every single breath.

©©©
I hope my words have really caught your ear . . .
So maybe . . . your mom won't have to shed a tear!

I am an ex-gang member and a drop-out **(a drop-out is one who disassociates himself from a gang through specific law enforcement sanctioned procedures)** of La Nuestra Familia/ La Nuestra Raza California Prison based gangs, and prior to that a member of the Northern California Nortenos (a CDCR prison disruptive group and statewide street gang under the control and direction of La Nuestra Familia/La Nuestra Raza*).* I was involved in some pretty rough stuff.

I was a gang member of some sort or another for the past thirty years. I have committed acts in the furtherance of these gangs over the years and have had control of two level III prison yards as OA (Overall authority). I have stabbed rival gang members, ordered stabbings and assaults, and been stabbed. I have been highly educated into the workings of the gang as well. Things like Nuestra Familia history, Aztec Culture, Weaponry (I am able to manufacture any of a number of weapons out of rolled up paper, thread from state issue laundry, and plastic wrap), Recruitment, Regimental Operations, The Fourteen Bonds and the Nuestra Raza Format among other things. I have risen through the ranks through-out the years and have had deep involvement in gang business

But prior to all of that, I was also present as a youngster (18 years old) and in the midst of one of the most violent and infamous prison riots in America, as I was doing two to ten years in one of the worst prisons in the United States at the time, the Penitentiary of New Mexico at Santa Fe. It was a menagerie of misfits with no classification system ensuring that inmates with the same level of sophistication and age be housed together. I was with lifers and extremely violent murderers and in the midst of an extremely violent environment. I witnessed, I experienced, and I survived **The New Mexico Prison Riot of 1980**. I believe these experiences along with my research do qualify me to speak on this subject. Maybe even a little over-qualified, wouldn't you think? Below is an article on the aforementioned prison riot.

New Mexico State Penitentiary Riot

From Wikipedia, the free encyclopedia

"The New Mexico Penitentiary Riot, which took place on February 2 and February 3, 1980, in the state's <u>maximum security prison</u> south of <u>Santa Fe</u>, was one of the most violent <u>prison riots</u> in the history of the American correctional system: 33 inmates died and more than 200 inmates were treated for injuries. None of the 12 officers taken hostage were killed, but seven were treated for injuries caused by beatings and rapes. This was the third major riot at the NM State Penitentiary, the first occurring on 19 July 1922 and the second on 15 June 1953."

"Author Roger Morris in The Devil's Butcher Shop: The New Mexico Prison Uprising (University of New Mexico Press, 1988) suggests the death toll may have been higher, as a number of bodies were incinerated or dismembered during the course of the mayhem."

Causes

"The causes of the New Mexico Penitentiary riot are well documented. Author R. Morris wrote that "the riot was a predictable incident based on an assessment of prison conditions".

"Prison overcrowding and inferior prison services, common problems in many correctional facilities, were major causes of the disturbance. On the night of the riot, there were 1,136 inmates in a prison designed for only 900. Prisoners were not adequately separated. Many were housed in communal dormitories that were unsanitary and served poor-quality food."

"Another major cause of the riot was the cancellation of educational, recreational and other rehabilitative programs that had run from 1970 to 1975. In that five-year period, the prison had been described as relatively calm. When the educational and recreational programs were stopped in 1975, prisoners had to be locked down for long periods. These conditions created strong feelings of deprivation

and discontent in the inmate population that would later lead to violence and disorder."

"Inconsistent policies and poor communications meant relations between officers and inmates were always in decline. These patterns have been described as paralleling trends in other U.S. prisons from the 1960s and 1970s, and as a factor that moved inmates away from solidarity in the 1960s to violence and fragmentation in the 1970s."

Snitch Game

"Due to a shortage of trained correctional staff, officers used a form of social manipulation called the "snitch game" to control uncooperative prisoners. Officers would simply label inmates who would not behave as informers."

"This tactic meant the "named" inmate would start being abused by fellow convicts. Often, prisoners would choose to become a "snitch" to get away from their tormentors. However, the practice hampered attempts to get accurate information from inmates. It also increased tensions within the prison, as inmates became even more suspicious of the officers and each other."

"Nevertheless, conditions were tolerated by New Mexico's state Governor Bruce King, Director of Prisons Felix Rodriguez and prison officials Robert Montoya and Manuel Koroneos. Warnings of an imminent riot were not heeded."

Hostages taken

"In the early morning of Saturday, February 2, 1980, two prisoners in south-side Dormitory E-2 overpowered an officer who had caught them drinking homemade liquor. Within minutes, four more of the 15 officers in the dormitory were also taken hostage. At this point the riot might have been contained; however, a fleeing officer left a set of keys behind."

"Soon, E-2 cell block was in the inmates' control. Prisoners using the captured keys now seized more officers as hostages, before releasing other inmates from their cells. Eventually, they were able to break into the prison's master-control center, giving them access to lock and door controls, weapons, and more key sets."

Violence ensues

"By mid-morning events had spiraled out of control within the cellblocks. Murder and violence had erupted. Gangs were fighting gangs, and a group of rioters led by some of the most dangerous inmates (who by now had been released from solitary confinement) decided to break into cell block 4, which housed the protective-custody unit. This held the snitches and those labeled as informers. But it also housed inmates who were vulnerable, mentally ill or convicted of sex crimes. Initially, the plan was to take revenge on the snitches, but the violence soon became indiscriminate."

"When the group reached cellblock 4, they found that they did not have keys to enter these cells. Unfortunately for the prisoners in protective custody, the rioters found blowtorches that had been brought into the prison as part of an ongoing construction project. They used these to cut through the bars over the next five hours. Locked in their cells, the segregated prisoners called to the State Police pleading for them to save them, but to no avail. Waiting officers decided to do nothing despite there being a back door to cellblock 4, which would have offered a way to free them."

"Meanwhile the rioters began taunting prison officials over the radio about what they are going to do to the men in cell block 4. But no action is taken. One official is heard to remark about the men in the segregation facility, "it's their ass". As dawn broke, an 'execution squad' finally cut through the grille and entered the block. The security panel controlling the cell doors was burned off. Victims were pulled from their cells to be tortured, dismembered, decapitated, or burned alive."

"During an edition of <u>BBC</u>'s <u>Timewatch</u> program, an eyewitness described the carnage in cell block 4:

> *'I was sighting on the guard tower opposite the custody unit. They lay this guy out on one of the cell doors. One of the prisoners then took a blowtorch and began cutting this guy apart. He was screaming all the time until they put the torch through his head.'*

Men were killed with piping, work tools and knives. One man was partially decapitated after being thrown over the second tier balcony with a noose around his neck. The corpse was then dragged down and hacked up. Fires had also begun raging unchecked throughout several parts of the prison."

Negotiations begin

"Talks to end the riot stalled throughout the first 24 hours. This was because neither the inmates nor the state had a single spokesperson. Eventually, inmates made 11 general demands concerned with basic prison conditions like overcrowding, inmate discipline, educational services and improving food. The prisoners also demanded to talk to independent federal officials and members of the news media."

"The officers who were held hostage were released after inmates met reporters. Some of the officers had been protected by inmates, but others had been brutally beaten and raped. Seven officers suffered severe injuries.

> *'One was tied to a chair. Another lay naked on a stretcher, blood pouring from a head wound. (Journal reporter).'*

Negotiations broke off again in the early hours of Sunday morning. State officials insisting no concessions had been made."

Inmates flee

"However, eighty prisoners, wanting no further part in the disturbances, fled to the baseball field seeking refuge at the fence where the <u>National Guard</u> had assembled."

"On Sunday morning, more inmates began to trickle out of the prison seeking refuge. Black inmates led the exodus from the smoldering cellblocks. These groups, large enough to defend themselves from other inmates, huddled together as smoke from the burned-out prison continued to drift across the recreation yard."

Order restored

"By mid-afternoon, 36 hours after the riot had begun; heavily armed State Police officers accompanied by National Guard servicemen entered the charred remains of the prison."

"Official sources state that at least 33 inmates died. Some overdosed on drugs, but most were brutally murdered. (Some sources cite a higher death toll). Twenty-three of the victims had been housed in the protective-custody unit. More than 200 inmates were treated for injuries sustained during the riot. After the surrender it took days before order was maintained enough to fully insure inmates could occupy the prison. National Guardsman over the next two nights threw lumber scraps from Santa Fe Lumber yards over the two layered fence into the Prison Yard to ensure inmates who escaped into the yard would not freeze in the near zero temperatures. Nevertheless rape, gang fights, and racial conflict continued to break out among the inmates."

Legacy

"A few inmates were prosecuted for crimes committed during the uprising, but according to author Roger Morris, most crimes went unpunished. The longest additional sentence given to any convict was nine years. Nationally known criminal defense lawyer <u>William L. Summers</u> lead the defense team in defending dozens of inmates

charged in the riot's aftermath. In 1982, Mr. Summers received the <u>National Association of Criminal Defense Lawyers</u>, Robert C. Heeney award, the highest award available to a criminal defense lawyer for his work in defending the inmates prosecuted with regard to the riot."

"After the riots, Governor King's administration resisted attempts to reform the prison. Actions were not settled until the administration of Governor <u>Toney Anaya</u> seven years later."

"Much of the evidence was lost or destroyed during and after the riot. One federal lawsuit that had been filed by an inmate was held up in the New Mexico prison system for almost two decades."

"However, systemic reforms after the riot were undertaken following the <u>Duran v. King</u> consent decree, which included implementation of the <u>Bureau Classification System</u> under Cabinet Secretary Joe Williams. This reform work has developed the modern correctional system in New Mexico."

"Situated within 20ft of the main control center, the prison library and its law collection remained relatively untouched.

http://en.wikipedia.org/wiki/New_Mexico_State_Penitentiary_riot

It was two in the morning on a Saturday night and the inmates housed in Dorm E-1 were just winding down and getting ready to call it a night (Saturdays and Sundays were late night TV days) as the guards would be in shortly to count and to lock down the T.V. Room. As I headed toward my rack, I noticed that several inmates were running around in the hallway with bandanas covering their faces and holding weapons. Then one ran up to the door, opened it with a key, and yelled, "Get up. It's a riot!" Our entire dorm mobilized and prepared by arming themselves with shanks and makeshift weapons. I secured an ax handle as a weapon, and found a gas mask as well. I was young and scared, but I followed my instincts and I survived the massacre.

At first it was all about breaking into the commissary and other areas of the prison, but once the pharmacy was broken into and inmates got a hold of the narcotics, all hell broke loose. People began to overdose and fight over possession of the drugs. Neighborhood and town members began fighting each other and other inmates began to settle old grudges. I saw things there that no ordinary human should ever experience. The carnage was beyond unbelievable and I witnessed it first-hand.

Each of the dormitories (there were 10 fifty man dorms in all) had a Correctional Officer hostage brought to them and held in his boxers, blindfolded, and hogtied on the floor. The guard in our dorm was continually being severely kicked and brutalized with weapons by inmates passing through. The level of inhumanity toward these men was unbelievable. Several of the officers were severely wounded as a result of the violence.

I went through cell block four about the time that the crazies rampaged through it and I could not believe the level of violence that was expended on the poor individuals that were housed there. One guy whom I had assaulted in my dorm with a lead pipe six months earlier was there (he had tried to pressure me because I was a youngster so I assaulted him) and when he saw me, he begged me to help him out of his cell. I simply scoffed at him and walked away. He died in the bloody aftermath. Today I truly regret not helping Jesse out of his cell that day. The body count and the way many of them were murdered was completely horrendous.

At the age of eighteen and with such a young mentality, I was pretty much traumatized by the brutality of all that I had seen. I don't think I was traumatized right then and there, as I was in shock most of the time, but the images stayed with me for a lifetime and definitely took their toll. One image that stays vivid in my mind today, three decades later, is that of a blood covered white inmate walking down the corridor carrying a butcher knife in one hand and the severed bloody arm of another man in the other. The look in this man's face is something I will not likely ever forget. It changed me forever as a man and I no longer had care or concern for the life of another human being.

As far as I was concerned, I had seen the worst of the worst when it comes to human interaction, and nothing more could ever shock me or surpass the evil I had witnessed. It would take over thirty years for me to come to terms with what I had seen and experienced in those few days of absolute carnage. From that day forward I was able to hurt others indiscriminately and without remorse or a second thought. Actually I justified the brutality of my assaults on others by minimizing it in comparison to the carnage I had witnessed.

I was paroled shortly after the riot and had horrible nightmares of what I had seen. Once paroled, I ran around acting out vicious and brutal behavior on those around me and those who crossed me. I quickly earned the reputation of been a nut who would cut you or bash your head in with a pipe for next to nothing at all. I always went to the extreme in matters of violence because as a matter of survival I wanted to leave such an impression that my intended victims would not even consider retaliation. I would leave them bloody and battered for the most minimal of reasons. I used knives, baseball bats, and lead pipes. That is . . . until I graduated to guns. But that's another story. Suffice it to say that I wouldn't hesitate to pull the trigger on anyone.

Tombstones and caskets . . .
The final reward . . .
It's all that is left . . .
For those who act hard.
©©©
Gangsters for life . . .
Playing the role . . .
Paying the price . . .
Selling their souls.
©©©
Ready for battle . . .
Ready to kill . . .
Vicious and mean . . .
Monsters for real.
©©©
Schooled by the game . . .
The game of hard knocks . . .
Seeking their fame . . .

Armed with a Glock.
©©©
When will it end?
How many must die?
Wasted away . . .
Living the lie?
©©©
Where can they go?
To secure their freedom?
What is your goal?
Join 'em . . . or beat 'em?
©©©

Thus my long road in and out of prisons and correctional institutions began. A road that would take me across several state lines, in the most brutal and isolated of prison settings, and eventually to here where I am now. A reformed gang member and drop out. One who is finally at peace with himself, and with God Almighty, but has yet to make amends to society, to his family, and to himself. This book is a step in that direction.

CHAPTER NINE

Why Do People Leave Gangs?

They do not know the ugly side of the gangster lifestyle, nor do most of them fully comprehend the consequences of choosing to follow that path. The lives wasted and destroyed, the impudent attitudes, the deaths, and even the deeper more serious involvement of gang activity. This is the reality! I lived it and loathed it. From young gang member to o'l time gangster to drop-out . . . a full 360. I used to think I was all that and then some. But to who? Myself? What did I know? To my peers? They were just as lost as I was. To society? Not hardly. For all of my false pride and arrogance my only reward was to spend over thirty years in and out of prison and to carry lifelong emotional and physical scars.

The word dignity (the quality or state of being worthy, honored, or esteemed) has no place in the world of gangs or in the make-up of a gang member, although most of them erroneously believe that they carry a measure of it within themselves. The fact is that most thugs believe that they have integrity, yet the lie, cheat, and kill indiscriminately. In their world it's "kill or be killed", so they have no room for the righteous and worthy attributes of a normal person with in a social setting, though they would like to think so.

Youngsters only the see the attention they receive from their peers when they "act a fool". Anything beyond that is unimportant. Immediate self-gratification becomes the most important and essential thing in their lives. They do not even realize what they are doing to themselves and before you know it . . . it's too late to have a change of heart and alter their course without serious repercussions.

It is unfortunate that most gang members do not see the folly of their ways until they are washed up and sitting in the S.H.U. forever. Life as they knew it has abruptly come to an end. They will marinate in an eight by ten cell 23 hours a day for the rest of their time, and for some that means the rest of their lives. That is unless they choose to drop-out and debrief. And believe me, they have by the hundreds. The S.N.Y.'s (special needs yards) are filled with drop-outs. And more than half the prisons with in the state of California are S.N.Y. prisons. Go figure!

"Seeking a haven from gang life, thousands of California inmates are choosing to live on 'sensitive-needs' yards. The demand is growing."

"Once upon a time, had they met on a prison yard, inmates Emilio Soto and Gerardo Fuentes might have sliced each other to pieces."

"Soto was a gang member from Stockton, Fuentes one from Los Angeles." Any little look that I thought was disrespectful or he thought was disrespectful," Fuentes said, "and it would have been on."

September 16, 2005|Sam Quinones | Times Staff Writer

All because they chose to accept the temporary false respect and honor bestowed upon them by those who don't really matter. It certainly is not a worthy endeavor . . . that's for sure . . . not by a long shot. Woe to those who have to figure this out that long hard way. They and their families suffer the consequences. So beware my young friend . . . before it's too late! Use this information I offer and the sources that are quoted and provided to do your own research and enlighten yourself.

Parents are also encouraged to use this information as a stepping stone toward education and awareness of the gangster lifestyle and its dangers and negative effects. No matter what you may believe, or are being told about gangs, the real truth is that they are criminals . . . nothing more. And they are bent on death and destruction. Prisons are full of them. They commit atrocities daily in a city near you in the name of some fictitious cause. They murder, they extort, and they infiltrate. It's what they do. What will you do?

The brutal truth of gang life is that the only way most gang members leave the gang is in a body bag. That is the reality. Some do manage to move on to a better, peaceful life. It might be because they reach a level of maturity that allows them to see the dangers of gang life in a different light. However when one disassociates from one of these gangs, he runs the risk of retaliation by the gang. He must take care not to put himself or his loved ones in harm's way. Most gangs have no qualms about hurting your family in order to get to you. If a drop-out has family or gets a good job and a home and he wants to protect those things, it sometimes requires relocation and assumed identities to avoid the repercussions of one's actions.

In some cases, the impetus to leave gang membership is more sudden—a serious injury or some hard time in jail can turn some gang members' lives around. Surviving a life threatening injury, especially one that is directly related to gang activity may cause some to have a change of heart. Or the life threatening injury could have been caused by one's own gang for whatever reason. Gangs are constantly cleaning themselves up and removing those who are no longer trusted or desirable. Many have left the gang they belonged to because they were ostracized and targeted for removal or assassination.

Some may find a new direction in religion and decide that their faith in God is much greater and much more important than their loyalty to a gang. A change of heart in the Christian meaning would require such a decision to disassociate one's self from the influence of the gang. That is one of the reasons that I chose to disassociate from the gang I belonged to. As a matter of Christian ethics, I could no longer participate in those types of activities.

Whatever the reason may be, the ultimate decision to leave a gang can bring long lasting repercussions. One must take into account that in order to be recognized as a drop-out by the authorities, one must have debriefed and participated in a state sanctioned observation period with ex-members of rival gangs. This is a long drawn out process and it targets you for assault and possible assassination, if you are identified as being a part of this. The process took me most of four years to complete.

And even then, many of those who drop out cannot leave the lifestyle behind. Thus the formation of new gangs has occurred within the Special Needs Yards of California's prisons. Some justify it as a way to protect one's self from the previous gang they belonged to. Gangs like the Northern Riders or the New Flowers are dropouts from La Nuestra Familia and Nuestra Raza. But in reality it is just that they are hesitant to leave their past behaviors behind. Others simply can't leave it alone, so they continue the behaviors they had before but now in a new environment. Post-dropout S.N.Y. gangs have become a major problem within the California prison system, as the following article relates:

FBI: Gang 'dropouts' pose threat

By MARIA INES ZAMUDIO • The Salinas Californian • May 21, 2008

The FBI has warned law enforcement agencies that two groups of ex-Norteño gang members gaining strength in the prison system could spur more violence in Monterey County and elsewhere in Northern California.

A May 5 classified report, intended only for gang-intelligence officers, says Norteño "dropout" groups such as Nuevo Flores (New Flowers) and Northern Riders pose an increasing threat on the streets of Monterey, Santa Clara, San Francisco, Sacramento and Mendocino counties as they gain influence within the state's lockups, attracting large 3numbers of recruits.

The groups are made up of ex-Norteños and former members of Nuestra Familia who've joined forces, in part, to offer each other protection from their former gangs. Once released from prison, the report says, these gang dropouts aspire to establish official territory in areas already occupied by Norteño and Sureño street gangs.

Their focus, however, is more on organized crime such as drug sales and car theft than on winning turf by force.

Norteños and Sureños, which mean "northerners" and "southerners" in Spanish, are the two major rival gang groupings in the Salinas area. Nuestra Familia leaders in prison direct Norteño gang activity at the street level, while Sureños answer to the Mexican Mafia, also a prison gang.

The FBI's threat-assessment report is based on gang activity on the streets and in prisons from 2004 through this year.

"We are still not sure how strong (Nuevo Flores) are," said Monterey County Gang Task Force Cmdr. Dino Bardoni. "(Nuevo Flores) are a byproduct of prison, just like the others (Mexican Mafia and Nuestra Familia)."

'Keeping an eye on them'

The report says Nuevo Flores is loosely organizing in neighborhoods throughout Northern California, working with Northern Riders. Salinas' police, however, say the groups haven't gotten a foothold in Monterey County, at least not yet.

"We are aware of them (Nuevo Flores), and we are keeping an eye on them," said Salinas police Cmdr. Kelly McMillin. "But they are not a big problem here."

Sgt. Mark Lazzarini, a supervisor for the Salinas Police Department's Violence Suppression Unit, agreed, saying Nuevo Flores hasn't been a factor in this year's shootings and homicides.

"It has nothing to do with the new gang," he said of the street violence. "What we've seen is typical north and south problems - the same problems this community has seen for years."

Lazzarini, who read the FBI report this week, said he hasn't encountered anyone who's admitted to being with Nuevo Flores in Salinas, though he said he knows the dropout group is in the city. He said there are about 2,500 Norteños and more than 1,000 Sureños in Salinas.

But with a "clean-house" order now in effect - in which active gang members receive an order to assault ex-gang members - from both

Norteño and Sureño gangs, this year's uptick in violence is likely to continue, local gang experts say.

So far this year, there have been 10 gang-related homicides in Salinas and 16 gang-related shootings, including those that didn't result in injuries.

Dropout boost growth

When an active gang member - either Norteño or Sureño - decides to leave the gang, his name is placed on a "no-good list," Lazzarini said. Anyone on this list may be a target for a violent assault, which can prompt dropouts to unite for protection.

The growth within Nuevo Flores and Northern Riders largely coincides with an increasing number of inmates being sent to "special needs" yards - also known as dropout yards - at state prisons, said Sgt. D. Silva, a gang expert at the California Department of Corrections and Rehabilitation who's worked with its gang intelligence department for 10 years.

CDCR is still not sure how many members are active in Nuevo Flores, in part, because the department has not been able to launch a full investigation, Silva said.

Nuevo Flores formed inside the "sensitive needs" yards at Calipatria State Prison and Mule Creek Correctional Facility in 1998, Silva said. Members used the name Nuevo Flores because its initials, NF, are the same as those of their former prison gang, Nuestra Familia. The name also suggests a new beginning, Silva said. "We don't know the structure of Nuevo Flores," he said. "But we have to keep in mind that they bring the influences from their former gangs."

Unlike Nuestra Familia, which follows a military structure with generals, captains and soldiers, Nuevo Flores has a looser structure, he said.

While the gang was organized to provide protection and financial gain inside prison, those motives are at work on the streets as some of the members begin parole, Silva said.

"They still want to gang-bang," he said. "They still have the same gang mentality." Inside prison, Nuevo Flores and Northern Riders get along with each other, Silva said, as there's not much difference between the two, except for the age of the members; Northern Riders are usually younger.

Prison status investigated

The CDCR's gang intelligence unit classifies both Nuevo Flores and Northern Riders as "disruptive groups" as opposed to prison gangs. A "disruptive group" consists of inmates who pose a threat to the physical safety of other inmates or prison staff members because of their activities, according to prison guidelines. Gang experts have not completed a full investigation to determine whether the groups should qualify as prison gangs, Silva said. Gang intelligence officers determine whether a "disruptive group" has grown into a prison gang by conducting a thorough investigation. They usually look for rank structure in the group, tattoos, and colors and whether the group started in prison. Once they have the report, it is sent to Sacramento, where it is determined whether a disruptive group is a prison gang, Silva said.

If Nuevo Flores and Northern Riders ultimately achieve this classification, they could become more organized both at the street and prison level and inflict more crime on communities as their memberships expand, Silva said. There are seven prison gangs in California: the Mexican Mafia, Nuestra Familia, Northern Structure, Black Guerilla Family, Nazi Low Riders, Aryan Brotherhood and the Texas Syndicate, said CDCR public affairs officer Paul Verke.

Of dropouts, the Salinas Police Department's Lazzarini said, "We have to remember that they (ex-gang members) are criminals. Just because they are no longer with the gang, it doesn't mean that they are going to become Boy Scouts."

CHAPTER TEN

How gangs promote themselves

"One of the growing trends amongst Hispanic gangsters is the promotion of their gangs through rap music. The "14th" track on the "17 Reasons" Black/Brown CD is called "North Side Soldier" by a rapper from SFM. The "Generation of United Nortenos" or G.U.N. and Darkroom Familia label also promote gang violence. Rap was at first considered "Black music" by Surenos. Surenos would only listen to Oldies. Now Sureno rap music groups are just as big as Norteno ones. A rapper from Darkroom Familia was indicted on a RICO statute and the Generation of United Nortenos (GUN) CD was also used against them. The escalating violence between Nortenos and Surenos in California and elsewhere is expected to continue for a long time. Police Officers, Corrections, and the public need to be aware of this historical feud if we are to ever hope to end the violence . . . ."

Gabe Morales
Author/Trainer/Gang Specialist
Owner-Gang Prevention Services

They say the game is on tight! But don't you believe it. They just want you to bite. The lure of easy money, fast cars, and faster women is what they sell you on. It looks good in the movies . . . it sounds good in the videos . . . it even has a good beat. Flashing all that bling (gold and diamonds), making all that scrilla (money), smoking big fat blunts (marijuana rolled in cigar leaves), acting like they are above the law. Yeah Right! It's all pure propaganda made up to excite and incite young people to buy what they are selling.

Even the real gangsters got on the bandwagon with their own CDs called Generation of United Nortenos (G.U.N.) and Seventeen Reasons. It was one of the most skillfully masterminded recruiting tools of our time. Meant to excite, intrigue, and recruit Nortenos in unprecedented numbers . . . and it worked! The masterminds behind G.U.N. were none other than La Nuestra Familia Prison Gang. G.U.N. was such a success that the F.B.I. pulled it from store shelves and outlawed it.

It was a plot, a ruse, thought up by the ruling elite and carried out by a ranking Nuestra Familia member who was released form Pelican Bay and was given the funds to produce it. Because of this, La Nuestra Familia's rule flourished in Northern California through recruited regiments of Nuestra Raza soldiers under the command of a Nuestra Familia member. Drugs, murder, and mayhem ruled the day. Youngsters were pumped up, ready to do the Nuestra Familia's bidding by killing Surenos and Bulldogs (a drop-out faction of the Norteno Prison disruptive group, specifically from Fresno and surrounding Fresno County towns.), selling drugs, and committing countless crimes. They were ready to join the regiments, but to the Nuestra Familia they were simply a means to an end. The enrichment of the ruling elite!

They were a tool . . . nothing more. Used to achieve the Nuestra Familias leaders' personal agendas. This is a prime example of how gangs use the power and influence of the mass media to exploit youngsters. Think about that the next time you sit down with your child to watch a violent gangster film, or as you sit idly by while your child listens to some savage gangsta lyrics. Look around in your neighborhood and you'll see the signs of gangster life. Some young thug balling out of control. But look quick because he won't be there for very long. Not to worry though because there will be another to take his place. Maybe your child. Think about that.

Generation of United Nortenos CD

Law enforcement has taken control of this set of CD's because of its content and the message within the lyrics used to recruit northern California gang members for La Nuestra Familia. It is no longer available for sale to the general public, and gang members having possession of the CD violates probation or parole laws.

"They're great to use for department training or playing for parents, educating them about the true purpose of gangster rap. If you've ever been asked to provide gang awareness training this item is a must have!"

"This CD helped influence a large federal investigation (Operation Black Widow) into the illegal activities of the prison gang La Nuestra Familia."

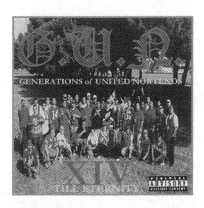

http://www.code3tactical.com/generation-of-united-norteno.aspx

"One of the growing trends amongst Hispanic gangsters is the promotion of their gangs through rap music. The "14th" track on the "17 Reasons" Black/Brown CD is called "North Side Soldier" by a rapper from SFM (San Francisco Mission District). The "Generation of United Norteños" or G.U.N. and Darkroom Familia label also promote gang violence. Rap was at first considered "Black music" by Sureños. Sureños would only listen to Oldies. Now Sureño rap music groups are just as big as Norteño ones. A rapper from Darkroom Familia was indicted on a RICO statute and the Generation of United Norteños (GUN) CD was also used against

them. The escalating violence between Norteños and Sureños in California and elsewhere is expected to continue for a long time. Police Officers, Corrections, and the public need to be aware of this historical feud if we are to ever hope to end the violence . . ."
http://www.offnews.info

Too many youngsters have fallen victim to this trend and have been laid by the wayside as they are led down the path of doom and destruction, in the wake of social permissiveness and moral decline. They seek alternatives and the gangster lifestyle is waiting in the wings to pluck them away from you. Without proper education and guidance regarding the adverse and negative effects that the gangster lifestyle poses, our youth are inevitably and inextricably being sucked into the vortex of the gang mentality and influence.

Gangsta Rap

"Gangsta rap is a subgenre of hip hop music that evolved from hardcore hip hop and purports to reflect urban crime and the violent lifestyles of inner-city youths. Lyrics in gangsta rap have varied from accurate reflections to fictionalized accounts. Gangsta is a non-rhotic pronunciation of the word gangster. The genre was pioneered in the mid-1980s by rappers such as Schoolly D and Ice-T, and was popularized in the later part of the 1980s by groups like N.W.A. After the national attention that Ice-T and N.W.A attracted in the late 1980s and early 1990s, gangsta rap became the most commercially lucrative subgenre of hip hop. Gangster rappers have been associated, or allegedly have ties with the Bloods or Crips gangs."

"The subject matter inherent in gangsta rap has caused a great deal of controversy. Criticism has come from both left wing and right wing commentators, and religious leaders, who have accused the genre of promoting violence, profanity, sex, homophobia, racism, promiscuity, misogyny, rape, street gangs, drive-by shootings, vandalism, thievery, drug dealing, alcohol abuse, substance abuse\ and materialism."
http://en.wikipedia.org/wiki/Gangsta_rap

What Is Gangsta Rap?

"Gangsta rap is a genre of hip-hop that reflects the violent lifestyles of inner-city youth. The genre was pioneered around 1983 by Ice T with songs like "Cold Winter Madness" and "Body Rock/Killers." Gangsta rap was popularized by illustrious rap groups like NWA and Boogie Down Productions in the late 80s."

Elements & Style:

"Gangsta rap revolves around aggressive lyrics and trunk-heavy beats. Despite its huge acceptance in the early 90s, gangsta rap has been condemned for its violent themes. Rappers often defend themselves by saying that they're only depicting actual inner-city struggles, not promoting it."

Gangsta Rap + Commercial Beats = Success:

"Gangsta rap gained commercial momentum after the release of Notorious B.I.G's Ready To Die. B.I.G. and his producer, Puff Daddy, meshed gritty narratives with polished pop beats entirely designed with clubs and pop charts in mind. Since then, the same blueprint has been reproduced over and over by today's rap artists."
http://rap.about.com/od/genresstyles/p/GangstaRap.htm

Any way you look at it, gangsta rap influences our youth in a big way and we just stand idly by and allow it to happen. It is seen as socially acceptable or at the very least, tolerable. Is it any wonder that our children look to those very avenues as guidance to live their lives? It's a huge money making scheme and everyone is jumping in on the action to get their issue, regardless of the negative influences that this genre creates. Everyone just turns a blind eye to the repercussions that come from allowing such music and ideology to run rampant in mainstream society. The threat is very real and it is consuming our youth at an escalating pace. Think about it.

Crime and Gangster Films

"Movies also contribute to the overall delinquency of today's youth. They portray gangsters as socially acceptable and even looked up to by others. Young people see these movies as ways to cut corners

in life and shortcuts to wealth and power, and then they try to emulate them."

"Crime and Gangster Films are developed around the sinister actions of criminals or gangsters, particularly bank robbers, underworld figures, or ruthless hoodlums who operate outside the law, stealing and violently murdering their way through life."

"Crime stories in this genre often highlight the life of a crime figure or a crime's victim(s). Or they glorify the rise and fall of a particular criminal(s), gang, bank robber, murderer or lawbreakers in personal power struggles or conflict with law and order figures, an underling or competitive colleague, or a rival gang. Headline-grabbing situations, real-life gangsters, or crime reports have often been used in crime films. Gangster/crime films are usually set in large, crowded cities, to provide a view of the secret world of the criminal: dark nightclubs or streets with lurid neon signs, fast cars, piles of cash, sleazy bars, contraband, seedy living quarters or rooming houses. Exotic locales for crimes often add an element of adventure and wealth. Writers dreamed up appropriate gangland jargon for the tales, such as "tommy guns" or "molls."

"Film gangsters are usually materialistic, street-smart, immoral, meglo-maniacal, and self-destructive. Rivalry with other criminals in gangster warfare is often a significant plot characteristic. Crime plots also include questions such as how the criminal will be apprehended by police, private eyes, special agents or lawful authorities, or mysteries such as who stole the valued object. They rise to power with a tough cruel facade while showing an ambitious desire for success and recognition, but underneath they can express sensitivity and gentleness."

"Gangster films are morality tales: Horatio Alger or 'pursuit of the American Dream' success stories turned upside down in which criminals live in an inverted dream world of success and wealth. Often from poor immigrant families, gangster characters often fall prey to crime in the pursuit of wealth, status, and material possessions (clothes and cars), because all other "normal" avenues

to the top are unavailable to them. Although they are doomed to failure and inevitable death (usually violent), criminals are sometimes portrayed as the victims of circumstance, because the stories are told from their point of view."
http://www.filmsite.org/crimefilms.html

Many of our youth's idols have money (or are portrayed as such), dress and act like thugs, and are, or at least seem to be, socially acceptable. Movies glorify these behaviors at the very least and add violence, greed, and the thug mentality into the mix. In short, without parental and social restraint on our youth, they fall prey to the pressures exerted by their peers and all the different media that espouse these ideas.

Gangs form due to the influence of the media.
"Gangs migrate into the minds and lives of young people through the mass media. The term "Mass media" refers here to the Internet, radio, television, commercial motion pictures, videos, CDs, and the press (newspapers, journals, and magazines) - what are referred to collectively as broadcast and print media. Their impact on the minds of our youth has been hotly debated. I believe media portrayals which glorify gang behavior do little to help reduce our youth's interest in gangs."

"You may recall our discussion of the role economic deprivation plays in the formation of gangs. The point of that discussion was that, being economically deprived, some youth will venture into illegal ways of earn an income. Movies and videos which show gang members enjoying the fruits of their illegal activities (i.e., drugs, sex, a nice apartment or house, money, cars, power, guns) suggest, in some children's minds, ways to reach the goal to which most American's aspire - financial success and all it entails. The ways in which that income is earned often entails the use of violence."

"Before the age of eighteen, the average American teen will have witnessed eighteen thousand simulated murders on TV. While staggering in number, more disturbing is the effect this steady diet of imaginary violence may have on America's youth."

"Over the past forty years, more than three thousand studies have investigated the connection between television violence and real violence . . . Though none conclude a direct cause and effect relationship, it becomes clear that watching television is one of a number of important factors affecting aggressive behavior. (Fanning, 1995)"

"By watching mass media portrayals of gang member behavior, some children learn of illegitimate ways to acquire goods and services. They learn how to lay in wait to "hit" (execute) someone. They learn what a drive-by-shooting looks like - how it's done and how to possibly get away without getting caught. If they watched American History X, they learned how to "curb" someone."

"If you didn't see American History X, here's what it shows - in full color and in all its gory detail. A Skinhead (a Caucasian gang known for its ideologically-based hatred of African-Americans and other minorities) is shown forcing an African-American youth to lay face-down in the street perpendicular to the curb. The youth's mouth is then forced open and pushed down until the curb is in his mouth. The skinhead then stomped on back of the young man's neck, fracturing his jaw, shattering his teeth, and breaking his neck."

"I mentioned earlier that the impact of the media on the minds of our youth is hotly debated. The debate goes like this . . ."

"There are those who believe only children who are predisposed to violence will be stimulated by it when shown in the media. Some believe otherwise non-violent children learn to be violent by watching violence, particularly when it is observed without the supervision of someone who explains that certain kinds of violence are inappropriate and wrong. Finally, there are those who believe violence in the media releases one's feelings of anger and violence by providing catharsis (in this case, a purging of one's own anger)."

"Which is right? I think they all are. I believe there are children who are raised in violence and who, when they observe violence or other gang activity in the media, view the media portrayal as

confirmation of what they already know. If you have a problem just put your fist in it and it will go away."

"I also believe there are unsupervised children who, fed a constant diet of television and rap music violence, begin to emulate it, particularly if there are others who are doing the same thing. Every child wants to be accepted. If I am rejected by the "good kids," perhaps the "bad kids" will want me if I act and think like they do. And there are those who feel frustration and anger who, after a media portrayal of violence, feel purged of such feelings."

"When I read about the relationship between violence in the media and violence among our youth I extrapolate the findings and think of them in regard to gangs. When it comes to the portrayal of gangs and gang members, the mass media sometimes go into great detail. They portray the language, dress, body movements, and look of a gang member - male and female. They show, in explicit detail, the crimes gang members commit - how drugs are sold, how to "shoot up" (inject drugs intravenously), how to free base, how to rape someone, how to stab or shoot someone, how to settle disputes using violence. The list is very long. The problem is that it is the wrong list in terms of socializing our youth into acceptable, legal behaviors."

"The impact of media portrayals of gangs and the activities of their members help us understand why gangs form, but sometimes gangs form by following in the footsteps of others."
http://people.missouristate.edu/MichaelCarlie/what_I_learned_about/GANGS/WHYFORM/mass_media_portrayals.htm

©©©
So you wanna be a gangsta and bang?
Well listen to the words that I say.
You might think that it's cool to be in a gang . . .
But there is a price that you'll pay.
©©©
It isn't just hanging and flagging the red . . .
Or the fake unity up on the block,

Sometimes it's seeing your friends wind up dead . . .
Blasted by some fool with a glock.
©©©
The cash is real easy and the girls are aplenty . . .
You might even sport some really nice wheels.
But what about the homie who got life with twenty?
Can you guess the way that he feels?
©©©
They buried the homie just the other day . . .
He died flagging his colors out by the pool.
When you see his mother, what do you say?
You swear your vengeance and promise to get that fool!
©©©
But she sheds a tear and holds you in her arms . . .
And begs you not to die . . . too many of you have.
She wishes her son's killer not one bit of harm . . .
And prays for all of you every day at mass.
©©©
Get right young man before it's too late . . .
And you wind up in a cold prison cell.
Or even worse, you meet your fate . . .
And wind up dead and . . . in hell.

Simply said, it's not all it's cracked up to be. Most don't realize this until it is much too late and they are sitting in a prison cell. By then it's usually really too late. Being accepted and having a sense of belonging can play a major role in the indoctrination of our young ones into the world of gang membership, and you can most certainly believe that existing gang members know this and utilize it to their advantage. This is the trend that we must address and make changes to. We cannot make the gangs stop doing what they are doing, but we can stop the flow of new members. Gangs sell a sense of belonging (however false it may be), and a sense of pride (false also) in their recruitment spiels, knowing that most young kids are looking for those things. That lack of family time and unity opens the doors for these thugs to influence and persuade our young. Being "one of the homies" is a sought after "pinnacle" in the neighborhoods across America as much as it is an entrance into the gang culture, and we would do well to realize this and do something to prevent it. It may start out as innocently as just hanging out with a few "homies" from the hood, but it simply and quickly progresses from there as it evolves into a sense of identity and turf. These are the traits that gangs look for in their prospects.

What's up witcha?
This life don't fit ya!
Yadda Mean?
It's low self-esteem.
©©©
Killing your brothers . . .
Pain to your mothers.
That's all it is . . .
When you dis,
©©©
This guy or that one.
Go get yo gun . . .
Shoot 'em up bang . . .
Cuz you in a gang!
©©©
Get caught up . . .
It don't stop . . .
Til you end up here.
Ain't pumpin' no fear . . .
©©©
Inside these walls.
Watch out, you'll fall . . .
Or you'll get beat up,
Messing wit me.
©©©
Fool can't you see?
This ain't even you . . .
It'll give you the blues . . .
And I will too!

CHAPTER ELEVEN

How do we save our children?

This is where we must first intervene on behalf of our youth. Before they get caught up in this identity and they build a wall around themselves. If we can nip it in the bud then, we save ourselves and our children much heartache later. I don't propose to know all the answers as all families are unique in their situations and conditions, but I do know that the lack of effort on our part as parents, grandparents, etc., will pretty much ensure the success of the gang culture.

Law enforcement cannot do it alone. They haven't even put a dent in it. Gangs continue to thrive and multiply. It has to start at home where the gangs look for new recruits. We must as individuals, assess our situations, however broad or unique they may be, and do what we must and what is right to respond to the onslaught of gangs. It may require outside help, research, and action, or even an introspective view of our own morals and standards (for we are the example that our children emulate).

The worst thing that we can do as parents is nothing at all. Our children deserve more than that. They deserve quality time and quality guidance. Every journey begins with one step, so please for your children's sake, take that first step. Don't wait for others around you to do something. Take the initiative and others will follow.

A diamond in the rough . . .
Trying to be tough,
Playing the game . . .
Gee . . . that's sure lame.
©©©
The game ain't about it . . .
Why would you doubt it?
Just look around you . . .
Don't be a fool.
©©©
Those who have played . . .
Have certainly paid.
Some with their lives . . .
Yet others survived,
©©©
Went to prison instead.
What's in your head?
Is it what you wan't?
For P.O.'s to haunt . . .
©©©
All that you do?
Who's fooling who?
Don't polish your stone . . .
Or go make your bones.
©©©
You might "Rest in peace" . . .
With others deceased.
Just turn away . . .
From the games that they play!
©©©

In order to help our young ones to avoid the perils I just described above, we must instill a sense of dignity and integrity in them. I imagine that statement is a lot easier said than done, but nonetheless, it can be done. It takes commitment on our part, but it is possible. Those two traits will help them to fend off the magnetic pull of the gangster lifestyle. However, we cannot pass on to our children traits that we do not possess.

It has taken me years of self-introspection and self-enlightenment to finally figure out what that was and how to apply it in my daily living. I actually thought I was dignified and had honor and respect in what I was doing as a gang member. I carried my head held high and was proud for being a Norteno and standing up for the so called "cause". I was so lost and now thanks to my personal relationship with my creator, I have fond my way back from the depths and degradation of the gangster lifestyle.

I finally figured out that I don't have all the answers. No . . . not even close! None of us do. That is why this world is in such a mess. The bible tells us that man's greatest wisdom is foolishness to our Heavenly Father. Through-out time man has brought calamity upon calamity onto this world and himself. Only trust and obedience in the Holy Scriptures, God's inspired word can free us of the bondage of our own self-serving interests. He gives us a guideline to follow so that we may live in happiness and joy.

Back when our parents were born, parenting skills were learned from the extended family. If parents, grandparents, aunts, and uncles didn't live in the same house, they usually lived within a few miles. They were always available to impart their considerable wisdom to the younger generation on the subjects of pregnancy, childbirth, and raising children. Now, we have become such a transient society; it is rare that the extended family is even in the same state! Since the late 20th and early 21st centuries, parents have had to learn creative ways to raise their children. We surf the Internet, read books, take classes, talk to our parents on the telephone, and make friends with parents who have "been there and done that." We then filter these things through our own morality, sensibilities, and personalities to make them work for our own families. Wouldn't it be easier if each baby arrived with an owner's manual attached?

Probably the most important and controversial parenting skill is discipline. We parents are conflicted over what type of discipline to apply at what time. Appropriate discipline for a two year-old might not be appropriate or effective for a 10 year-old or a teenager. The most important piece of the discipline puzzle is determining who is in charge: the parents or the child. This may sound simple, but in this day and age, the answer isn't always clear.

The fear of hurting a child's feelings or crushing his spirit coerces many parents into allowing their children to rule the roost. Children need firm boundaries that come from clear and consistent parental discipline. Whether the method is redirection, time-outs, loss of privileges, grounding, extra chores, or spanking, it is crucial that we embrace our role to train our children to become moral, respectable adults.

The ability to recognize what we teach our children is one parenting skill from which we can all benefit. From the moment our children are born, they are learning from us. They learn that if they cry, we respond. If they pull our hair, we say, "ouch." If they throw their cup on the floor, we pick it up. As time goes on, we also teach them to walk, talk, get dressed, and say their A-B-C's. As parents, we also have the responsibility to teach our children morals and values. We cannot depend solely on the schools to fulfill this important duty. At some point during early childhood, parents must make a decision on how to handle a child's formal education.

A child's educational success is not always dependent upon where he attends school, but how involved his parents are in his education. Children bring us much joy and much responsibility. Taking the time to plan ahead can take some of the stress and worry out of raising them.

Parental neglect and disassociation have risen considerably in recent decades. This unfortunate trend has had a profound destabilizing effect on the home environment and the relationships between parents and their children. Lack of respect is more common today, as well as children assaulting their parents. Poor parental efforts, a lack of discipline, and deep seated social permissiveness and complacency bear the blame for the attitudes and behavior of today's youth. Kids have no respect for their parents, no respect for authority, and most certainly no respect for themselves.

But the sad fact is that our children are crying out. They need us . . . they need fathers to teach them honor and respect . . . they need mothers to nurture and love them . . . they need both to teach them morals, values, and principles. They need tempered discipline to teach them right from wrong. They need the family unit to teach them cooperation and responsibility. The absence of these primary needs has forced our children to adapt and do what they can with-out us. To seek outside acceptance and start to rebel. It's their way of emotional survival. They don't know any better because no one has taught them any better.

We need to take the time to stand in, be firm yet loving, and to instill the necessary tools, not only in our children, but in ourselves as well. We need to return to the traditional values of a half century past. Those things that have been cast by the wayside for the sake of modernism. Let's not be content to leave the support of our children to Social Programs. Or the raising of our children to the juvenile system and the courts. Let's not be willing to sacrifice family for personal gratification.

Let's work hard and keep our kids in school, off of drugs, sexually moral, and out of gangs. They are the future of this world and they are headed in the wrong direction. Let's fend off the very culture that we have allowed to come into existence and prevail. One that is poisoning our kids and killing them with drugs, hatred, and violence. Let's just be good, decent, hard-working people and raise our families to do the right thing, great or small, even when no one is looking.

Let's be the backbone of our communities, our neighborhoods, and our streets. Let's wake up and stop making excuses. Let's teach our youth about good clean and moral fun without the presence of gangs, violence, or drugs. Let's go to church together and eat dinner together as a family. Let's share quality time with one another. Let's come together as a neighborhood, get to know our neighbors, and be social and kind. This has all been left by the wayside. Isn't it time to reclaim it? I think so

Stand firm with your children about the sort of music they listen to . . . about the way they dress . . . about their expectations in school. Emphasize family time, family discussions, and family activities. Family unity is important and builds character on our children. Teach them, or at the very least encourage them, towards good Christian ethics. Always listen to your children for sometimes they cry out and we don't listen or can't seem to hear. Take time out of your day for your children. These things really aren't that hard. They are just low on one's list of priorities. We need to re-prioritize according to our values and our principles. We are their mentors and their examples, so we need to be the best that we can be at that. Don't leave that job up to others in the community.

It may be time consuming taking in the busy schedules of today's economic structure, but it is well worth the effort and will save you and your young ones much heartache in the future. Take the time and re-organize your family agenda. I came from a well to do family and because I was left to my own devices for much of the time, I began to look to the neighborhood for fulfillment of the things I was not getting at home. Attention . . . acceptance . . . quality time . . . praise . . . etc.

Teach Your Child How to Make Good Choices

"As children grow so do the number of choices they have to make. The choices will begin just as soon as they start school and will continue to grow in complexity as your child matures. What does it take to make a choice? Making a choice takes a balance of self-confidence and the mental ability to think through the consequences of your decision. Therefore, teaching a child to make good choices will benefit them for years to come and will definitely set your child in the right direction."

"Children should be eased into decision-making at an early age. Below is a breakdown of each age group and the suggested amount of choices that should or will be presented in their lives."

Preschool
"When children are in this age group it is a great time to introduce decision-making to your child, by offering simple daily choices to your child. Start in the morning by picking out two shirts for your child and ask them which one they would like to wear for the day. Throughout the day you can continue with small choices, "Would you like an apple or banana for a snack today? If they are unsure of which to pick, let them know it's okay to take their time and just pick one, when you are giving your child a decision to make be sure to allow them to make the choice, otherwise they may depend on you to make all their choices."

"Once your children get the hang of making decisions for themselves, offer them choices that affect the entire family as well. Do you think

we should have rice or potatoes for supper? Or which flowers should we plant in the front lawn, the white ones or the red ones? This gives your child the sense of family contribution and self-worth, their opinion is important to the family unit."

Main points to address:

- *Encourage them to learn decision-making skills early, would you like an apple or cheese for a snack today?*
- *Allow them to choose between only two different objects at a time (which of these shirts would you like to wear today?)*
- *Once they can make decisions for themselves, allow them to make decisions that affect the entire family.*

Grades K-3rd
"As most parents know, teaching through example is a very good starting point to teaching our children the values we want to instill in them. Talking about good choices is your next best tool, explain to your child what a good decision is. A good decision is one that results in more good than harm, considers the feelings of other, is selfless, follows the rules, and is positive and beneficial."

"At this stage of childhood children will make a number of choices that we aren't happy with or make us turn the other cheek and wonder if that was actually our child. Allow children to make these choices, good or bad, and when the choice comes up that is not so good this is the perfect opportunity to talk about choices with your child. "The choice you made to spit in the house was not an appropriate decision; let's talk about choices and how they affect you and the people around you."

Main points to address:

- *Teach internal control*
- *Ask questions instead of giving directions.*
- *Be a good example.*
- *Allow children to make mistakes*

- *This teaches them how to handle their errors in the future.*
- *Be compassionate to your child.*

Grades 4th-6th

"It's an essential feeling to know that you are needed or of importance. Normally we gain this understanding by the jobs we do and the positions we hold in society or our home life. It is also a very important feeling for children. This not only helps children to make the right decision when they have choices presented to them, but this ensures they will make the right choice. Think of how important we felt once we became parents, all our choices changed in the blink of an eye, because someone else needed us. This rings true for this age group as well. Give your child a responsibility that makes them feel they are making a difference, not simply taking out the trash, but something that makes them feel they are contributing something important. For example, taking care of the family pet, making sure the wild birds have food, etc."

"Tell your children the truth about a variety of important issues, especially when they ask. Children that feel as though they are being misled or lied to from their parents, they don't feel as though they are important enough or not smart enough to handle the truth. Tell the truth about the effects of drugs and alcohol, one hit from certain drugs can kill you or make you addicted, which leads to worse things in your life, etc."

"Encourage your child to form positive friendships, see How to Form Positive Relationships on this site, children are more than 50% likely to make the same choices their closest friends make, therefore the friends they have and the choices their friends make will make a huge difference in your child's decision making."

"One other very important step is to talk to your children about the effects of negative choices and the effects of positive choices, "If Oprah Winfrey never made the choice to go to college she may not be the highest paid woman in television history. The more open you are now with your children, the better and stronger

the lines of communication when they get to an age where peer pressure, bad choices and the negativity of the teenage years will be in abundance."

Main points to address:

- *Give them a responsibility*
- *Helps to show that they can do something of importance and helps promote self-discipline.*
- *Establish boundaries.*
- *Tell them the truth about drugs and other harmful substances that might be a part of their choice making sometime in the future.*
- *Help them choose positive friendships.*

http://www.teachkidshow.com

ACCEPTANCE-IS IT WORTH IT???

Our youth are being misled and are much too willing to bear the costs, willing to lose, and willing to get burned for the sake of acceptance. Only knowledge taught and values instilled can give them the tools that are needed to fend off or step away from the lure of gangs. Without these tools our children are being lured away to the world of gangsta rap, gangster movies, the thug mentality, and the gang culture. It's all around them. They can't help but to see and hear it. Prime prospects for easy recruitment.

There is increasing proof that exposure to the permissive attitudes on the various media outlets can shape one's mental and moral blueprint in a negative fashion and eventually affects one's behavior. Adolescents who have high levels of exposure (don't they all?) to these permissive attitudes are more likely to step into criminality, into gangs, and into prison, than those who have little or no exposure. Critical attention should be given to the magazines, music, video games, televisions, and the internet to gauge your child's exposure to this type of dangerous content. These venues are interlaced with violence, permissiveness, and immorality. They glorify the thug mentality for the sake of money, without concern to the repercussions, which wreak havoc on a child's values and principles.

Gang Prevention

"Gang prevention is a problem we have been struggling with for a long time, but it seems that the more effort that goes into this cause, the worse the problem seems to escalate. Is it a problem for government or does the solution lies with all of us?"

"Even if the problem is one for everyone to deal with where do we begin? Has the problem with gangs spiraled to such a degree that us as individuals are helpless to eradicate it. Or is it because we think we cannot do much to prevent the situation that we just don't."

"Although gangs are a huge burden on society, we don't often know a lot about it. To stop gangs, it is imperative to know gangs better, their ways of communication and their behaviors. The police seem to be swamped with crimes committed by gangs and always need the help of everyone to let them know when there are any gang related activities going on."

"A gang is a group of people with a common idea. The gang will be identified by its name, colors and all members will be required to commit a crime. Because gang members usually come from bad homes and poor neighborhoods they find acceptance and support in their gangs. Their feelings towards their fellow gang mates can be compared to that of family and therefore they will do anything their gangs require."

"Starting to eradicate gang formation begins by looking at why people join gangs in the first place. Because gangs are the result of people being in bad situations financially and family wise, a plan to mitigate such social problems must be included in gang prevention. More employment opportunities must exist for young people and they should receive acceptance and support elsewhere, and not from gangs."

"Gang prevention begins at home when you suspect that a member of your family or a neighbor is a gangster. The signs often include a change in dress style, secret behavior and increase in money and possessions. If you suspect that a person is involved in such activity it is our duty to acknowledge it and report it. A problem only increases when you bury it and pretend it does not exist. You may even discover that gang problems are closer to home than what you think."

"Strategies For Gang Prevention: You have to try to make sure that young people in your family occupy their time with activities that are wholesome and productive, don't just allow them to hang around on street corners, the devil makes work for idle hands, make sure that they are involved with organized sports, hobbies and after school activities, these are all excellent ways to fill a young person's time and make them feel a part of a community."

"The biggest supporters of gang prevention are faith-based organization such as churches and NGO's. Their crime prevention efforts in general are outstanding and because they are mainly aimed at the youth, gang prevention becomes a cause at the top of their lists. Believing that young people have a better chance of being rehabilitated and reformed if they are given positive activities, they take a more direct role in working with young people."

"Gang members need to realize that gangs only bring a wasted future and certainly are no solution. Gang prevention should deal with the individual involved in order for them to have hope for a better life."

http://ezinearticleds.com/?GangPrevention-Strategies
David M. Walters

An adolescent's acceptance of these negative factors as well as our passive acquiescence leads to an isolated existence in an environment where survival of the strongest and most vicious is the order of the day. Where gang politics, turf wars, racial hatred, and violence is a part of everyday life. Where on can be snuffed out at a moment's notice, for the pettiest of reasons. Where one's life holds little or no value. We must fully comprehend the finality of this. Once you are dead, there is nothing else. Likewise once a child is in a gang they are pretty much dead to everything else, for nothing else matters but the gang. It's a hard reality, but it is definitely a reality that destroys.

I speak in hindsight, for I have done the years . . . I have survived the battles . . . I have dealt with the politics . . . I have experienced the hatred . . . the violence . . . and I carry the scars. Some you can see, others you cannot. Those are deeply imbedded, but they are constant reminders of my past transgressions. I live a life filled with regrets of a life gone so very wrong, for so very long. Of wasted years gone by, away from loved ones. And of emotional pain I've caused them.

I offer hindsight in an effort to make things right with myself and my loving creator, and as a warning of things to come for those who do nothing to stop the madness. A madness that brings results that is profoundly final for many. It's too late for those who have lost their lives to death or to life sentences. Too late to turn back the clock, for their fate is sealed and irreversible.

But it is not too late for many if they heed the warning, accept the insight, and move forward in a positive progressive journey. Do not follow the path of those lost souls and end up on death row, doing life, or at the dying end of a losing battle. Those lost, never envisioned that their lives would bring them to their misery. It just happened and I am here to tell you that every one of them truly wish that their lives would have been different. They all just put up a façade of bravado for their homies.

So please take heed and make changes now. Don't wait until you are lost or until one of your loved ones or a child you know is sitting in a cell. Reach out. Don't regret choices in hindsight, instead make choices with foresight. Don't let your young ones get caught up in the game . . . the politics . . . or in the gang culture. Life in prison sucks and life in the S.H.U. is a whole lot worse. Believe me when I say that. I spent many years there . . . and getting there was really easy. We need to teach those at risk that acceptance is not the way to go, but rather perseverance and persistence.

Living in the Hood

"A 'hood, also known as a ghetto, is a specific area where people sharing a similar ethnic or racial background live. The word '"hood" is essentially the slang alternative for neighborhood, although it has come to mean much more. For example, '"hood" now brings to mind a poverty-stricken area that is within the confines of an urban area. In contrast, poor neighborhoods in rural areas are often referred to as rural ghettos rather than 'hoods. Traditionally, the word 'hood referred to areas where the main population was African American. In areas where a lot of Hispanic immigrants have settled, the areas are often called barrios, the Spanish word for neighborhood."

"The 'hood" is a term often used by rappers to refer to their place of birth or to a place where they have lived a good part of their life. In rap songs, this place is often associated with poverty and crime, although that is not always the case in real life. People who grew up in the 'hood sometime dislike "outsiders" using the term to refer to the same neighborhood. Somehow, the word '"hood" conveys a sense of brotherhood reserved to those who actually experienced the place and the community. In some areas, the word '"hood" is politically incorrect term believed to have elitist or racial overtones."

"If we are to believe songs, the 'hood is an area where "gangsta culture" is very much alive, and where organized crime, the drug trade, and corrupt police forces are customary. The 'hood is not a place where you want to be, but a place you can be proud of escaping from. Rappers often use the word 'hood as a way of bringing back memories of a difficult past that has long been overcome. Boyz n the Hood is a 1991 film that is often cited as an example of "culturally significant" art. The film explores the lives of several young men living in South Central Los Angeles, an area well-known for its high crime level. Some other places that are commonly referred to as "the 'hood" are Brooklyn and South Bronx, parts of Houston, and Philadelphia (Philly)."
http://www.wisegeek.com

©©©
Living in the hood . . .
Up to no good!
What about you?
What do you do?
©©©
I'm stuck in here . . .
With hatred and fear.
You did the right thing . . .
You split the scene.
©©©
Me . . . I stuck around . . .
Cause I'm a hood hound.
You went to school . . .
Now you're living real cool.
©©©
I joined a gang . . .
Decided to bang.
You drive a Jag . . .
Have a nice house.
©©©
I sit here in prison . . .
My roommate's a mouse.
You have nice clothes . . .
And a life that you love.
©©©
I live a life . . .
That's hella rough.
Stuck in the hood . . .
Up to no good!

Not everyone who gets involved with gangs lives in "the hood", but it is most often portrayed as the center of gang activity and the epicenter of the gang culture. Actually, the fact is that gang members come from all walks of life. It isn't the influence of the hood that is solely responsible for the making of gangsters because good, productive people come out of the hood all the time. It is what is in the person and the tools that are at his disposal that determines where that person will go in life. Anyone can possess the tools that can help fend off bad habits, bad choices, and help them to become a positive member of society. Most people just don't take the time to learn what is needed to do so, or to teach their children these things.

I have heard countless stories during my days in the prison system where gangsters blame the hood, their environment, and the way they were raised for the way that they are and who they have become. These are simply excuses and not very good ones at that . . . cop outs for being a failure. I said those same things. But the one thing that I or any of those other guys didn't do was take responsibility for our own actions. It was always someone else's fault. The cold hard reality is that each one of us has to take responsibility for who we are and what we do. We all make choices every day, some good and some bad, but the bottom line is that we are responsible. No one else is. Those choices will most likely have a profound effect on our lives and the lives of those around us.

I'm sure that there are outside factors that come into play in our daily decision making, but for the most part it is our actions that will determine an outcome. It all comes down to choices. If we make uninformed decisions without the proper education and enlightenment, we usually do the wrong thing. Our choices mold us into who we are and set the direction that we are going to take in life. Isn't it worth a little effort on our part? Since our choices are so far-reaching, wouldn't it make sense to choose wisely and according to proper values and principles? I think so!

Many people have come from the hood, the barrio, and the projects, and have risen above their circumstances to become successful, productive people. They simply did not allow their environment to dictate what their lives would become. They chose to be proactive and make choices that were in line with their values and principles. It probably wasn't easy, in fact probably far from it. They avoided the neighborhood thugs, went to school, developed useful habits, and moved forward. Unfortunately, that is the exception rather than the rule. Too many youngsters in these socio-economic areas fall by the wayside, choosing the easy way and following the crowd . . . the path of least resistance.

"A family is a place where minds come in contact with one another. If these minds love one another the home will be as beautiful as a flower garden. But if these minds get out of harmony with one another it is like a storm that plays havoc with the garden."
—Buddha

One does not really appreciate the love, unity, and support of family until it is gone. Instead we all take the family unit for granted. What we all need to do is cherish our family as loved ones and who they are to us. Those who love us without condition or price. And in doing so, we need to live up to our own responsibilities within the family unit. It is virtually impossible not to be a member of a family.

Yet, how families influence and are influenced by one another is as numerous as the stars up in the sky. There are so many intangibles involved in each families daily interactions. In some cases, and at some times, families function in such a way that children's growth is positive and there is optimal development. In other cases, however, individual and socioeconomic forces compromise the family's ability to provide a supportive environment for their children. This is where the gangs come in, as the children turn to outside sources of comfort and acceptance.

There are several ways to consider how family dynamics affect child outcome. We should love and guide our children with disciplined temperance and affection. We should take the time to listen to them . . . interact with them . . . value their thoughts . . . answer their questions . . . give them counsel . . . and instill morals, values, sound principles, and ethics. Sons and daughters should honor and respect their parents and siblings, and should love them without condition and heed their guidance. Let's not forsake these things for the sake of expediency, rebellion, and greed. Too many lives have already been wasted and lost to the gangsters.

Families are complex, and at times confusing and puzzling as any family member can attest to. Landesman, Jaccard, and Gunderson (1991) have proposed that families are responsible for providing structure and care in six domains: (1) physical development and health, (2) emotional development and well-being, (3) social development, (4) cognitive development, (5) moral and spiritual development, and (6) cultural and aesthetic development. But how do families go about organizing their busy lives in order to fulfill all these demands? One way to tackle the complexity of the issue is to consider processes that are developmentally sensitive and reflect overall family organization. It takes some effort on our part, but it is definitely worth it.

So let's teach our children to face life head on, to overcome in the face of adversity, and to succeed in all of their endeavors. Let's teach them to be winners . . . not losers in this game of life. Let's give them the tools that they need to succeed. Let's quit acting as if we have some sort of deficiency and because of that, we are not able to turn this terror around . . . because we can! All it takes is some effort on our part. One parent at a time, one neighborhood adult at a time, one Christian at a time, and one brother or sister at a time.

Your Teen's Friends:

Peer Influence & Peer Relationships

Teens want to be with people their own age—their peers. During adolescence, teens spend more time with their peers and without parental supervision. With peers, teens can be both connected and independent, as they break away from their parents' images of them and develop identities of their own. While many families help teens in feeling proud and confident of their unique traits, backgrounds, and abilities, peers are often more accepting of the feelings, thoughts, and actions associated with the teen's search for self-identity. The influence of peers—whether positive or negative—is of critical importance in your teen's life. Whether you like it or not, the opinions of your child's peers often carry more weight than yours.

Positive Peer Pressure

The ability to develop healthy friendships and peer relationships depends on a teen's self-identity, self-esteem, and self-reliance. At its best, peer pressure can mobilize your teen's energy, motivate for success, and encourage your teen to conform to healthy behavior. Peers can and do act as positive role models. Peers can and do demonstrate appropriate social behaviors. Peers often listen to, accept, and understand the frustrations, challenges, and concerns associated with being a teenager.

Negative Peer Pressure

The need for acceptance, approval, and belonging is vital during the teen years. Teens who feel isolated or rejected by their peers—or in their family—are more likely to engage in risky behaviors in order to fit in with a group. In such situations, peer pressure can impair good judgment and fuel risk-taking behavior, drawing a teen away from the family and positive influences and luring into dangerous activities. For example, teens with ADHD, learning differences or disabilities are often rejected due to their age-inappropriate behavior, and thus are more likely to associate with other rejected and/or delinquent peers. Some experts believe that teenage girls frequently enter into sexual relationships when what they are seeking is acceptance, approval, and love. A powerful negative peer influence can motivate a teen to make choices and engage in behavior that his or her values might otherwise reject. Some teens will risk being grounded, losing their parents' trust, or even facing jail time, just to try and fit in or feel like they have a group of friends they can identify with and who accept them. Sometimes, teens will change the way they dress, their friends, give up their values or create new ones, depending on the people they hang around with.

Some teens harbor secret lives governed by the influence of their peers. Some—including those who appear to be well-behaved, high-achieving teens when they are with adults—engage in negative, even dangerous behavior when with their peers. Once influenced, teens may continue the slide into problems with the law, substance abuse, school problems, authority defiance, gang involvement, etc. If your teen associates with people who are using drugs or displaying self-destructive behaviors, then your child is probably doing the same.

Encourage Healthy and Positive Relationships

It is important to encourage friendships among teens. We all want our children to be with persons who will have a positive influence, and stay away from persons who will encourage or engage in harmful, destructive, immoral, or illegal activities. Parents can support positive peer relationships by giving their teenagers their love, time, boundaries, and encouragement to think for themselves.

Specifically, parents can show support by:

Having a positive relationship with your teen. When parent-teen interactions are characterized by warmth, kindness, consistency, respect, and love, the relationship will flourish, as will the teen's self-esteem, mental health, spirituality, and social skills. Being genuinely interested in your teen's activities. This allows parents to know their teen's friends and to monitor behavior, which is crucial in keeping teens out of trouble. When misbehavior does occur, parents who have involved their children in setting family rules and consequences can expect less flack from their children as they calmly enforce the rules. Parents who, together with their children, set firm boundaries and high expectations may find that their children's abilities to live up to those expectations grow. Encouraging independent thought and expression. In this way, teens can develop a healthy sense of self and an enhanced ability to resist peer pressure.

When Parents Don't Approve

You may not be comfortable about your son or daughter's choice of friends or peer group. This may be because of their image, negative attitudes, or serious behaviors (such as alcohol use, drug use, truancy, violence, sexual behaviors). Here are some suggestions: Get to know the friends of your teen. Learn their names, invite them into your home so you can talk and listen to them, and introduce yourself to their parents. Do not attack your child's friends. Remember that criticizing your teen's choice of friends is like a personal attack. Help your teen understand the difference between image (expressions of youth culture) and identity (who he or she is). Keep the lines of communication open and find out why these friends are important to your teenager. Check whether your concerns about their friends are real and important. If you believe your concerns are serious, talk to your teenager about behavior and choices—not the friends. Encourage your teen's independence by supporting decision-making based on principles and not other people. Let your teen know of your concerns and feelings. Encourage reflective thinking by helping your teen think about his or her actions in advance and discussing immediate and long-term consequences of risky behavior. Remember that we all learn valuable lessons from mistakes.

No matter what kind of peer influence your teen faces, he or she must learn how to balance the value of going along with the crowd (connection) against the importance of making principle-based decisions (independence). And you must ensure that your teen knows that he or she is loved and valued as an individual at home.

"Dignity is a term used in moral, ethical, and political discussions to signify that a being has an innate right to respect and ethical treatment. It is an extension of the Enlightenment-era concepts of inherent, inalienable rights. Dignity is generally proscriptive and cautionary: for example in politics it is usually used to critique the treatment of oppressed and vulnerable groups and peoples, but it has also been extended to apply to cultures and sub-cultures, religious beliefs and ideals, animals used for food or research, and even plants."

"The English word "dignity" comes from Latin dignitas by way of French dignité. In ordinary usage it denotes respect and status, and it is often used to suggest that someone is not receiving a proper degree of respect, or even that they are failing to treat themselves with proper self-respect. There is also a long history of special philosophical use of this term. However, it is rarely defined outright in political, legal, and scientific discussions. International proclamations have thus far left dignity undefined, and scientific commentators, such as those arguing against genetic research and algeny, cite dignity as a reason but are ambiguous about its application."

"According to Arthur Schopenhauer objective definition of dignity is opinion of others about our worth and subjective definition of dignity is our fear from this opinion of others."
From Wikipedia, the free encyclopedia

Dignity . . .
Do you know what that be?
It's being honest . . .
Not being "on us"
©©©
Taking away . . .
From loved ones each day.
It's being true . . .
To those who love you,
©©©
And doing what's right . . .
Not trying to fight . . .
For a name or a turf.
Your dignity deserves . . .
©©©
Better than that . . .
That's just an act.
You should be caring . . .
Loving and sharing,
©©©
Not saggin' and raggin' . . .
Or hangin' and bangin'.
Dignity doesn't . . .
Mean fighting and fussing.
©©©
It gives you pride . . .
That doesn't deride . . .
The man that you are . . .
Dignity . . . you could go far!
©©©

Learning self-worth (dignity) and honor (integrity) will help our young ones to rise above the peer pressure and to have confidence to stand on their own two feet in the face of adversity. Knowing and living these principles will help them to see through the false ideologies that are espoused in the gang culture. Gangs use the very same words: Dignity, integrity, honor, loyalty, and discipline to dress up their corrupt ways and to lure young impressionable youths to their cause. I myself have used such spiel to recruit new members into La Nuestra Raza. It is these things that young people are looking for and they inevitably find it with those who corrupt those principles, making them simple lies and a facade used to disguise their real agenda . . . the agenda of the real Mexican Gangster.

These thugs could care less about any words that come out of their mouth to pull a youngster. They are just a means to an end to them. And they care even less about the young recruits that they bring into the fold. They are simply seen as torpedoes (soldiers), tools of the trade, and very much expendable. These guys sit up in the S.H.U.'s and make decisions that enrich them and their inner circle without care or concern for the soldier's welfare. They rule with an iron fist and will order a member to be killed for the smallest of reasons. It's literally their way or no way. Look at Mikeo Castillo. He was killed simply because they thought that he was not bringing in enough money so therefore, he had to be skimming off the top. He was a loyal NF soldier and when the police told him that he was targeted for assassination, he scoffed at them, because he didn't believe that his actions warranted such an order. He simply thought that the police were trying to turn him.

Everyone murdered at the hands of the Nuestra Familia leaders was either a Norteno, a member of the subordinate La Nuestra Raza, or a member of La Nuestra Familia, or a rival gang member. Some were even ranking members as in the case of Robert "Brown Bob" Viramontes (an NF General who upset the powers that be by talking to MADD [mothers against drunk driving] about gang prevention). On April 19, 1999, the Nuestra Familia murdered 20 year gang veteran ROBERT "Brown Bob," VIRAMONTES in his garage. NF leaders in Pelican Bay state prison ordered the hit because Viramontes was no longer involving himself in crime. And this kind of story repeats itself through-out the history of the Nuestra Familia as well as all of the other prison gangs. If left unchecked, you can pretty much bet that most of our youth will be headed in that direction. Are you willing to stand idly by and allow your loved one to head down the path of death and destruction? The direction of the Mexican Gangster.

©©©
Mexican gangster . . .
Up in the S.H.U.
Being a prankster . . .
Trying to fool you.
©©©
He's doing life . . .
Got nothing to lose.
Tell you some lies . . .
Mixed in with truth.
©©©
That's how he does it . . .
Just plays the game.
Plays you for stupid . . .
So he can gain.
©©©
It ain't about you . . .
It's about him.
You do what you do . . .
So he can win.
©©©
He comes up fat . . .
Locked in a cell.
You take the rap . . .
Go straight to hell.
©©©
Once you're used up . . .
He'll throw you away.
There was never no love . . .
You just got played!
©©©

And that's pretty much how it is. Its big business for those in leadership positions and the rest are just expendable commodities. No one realizes this going in because they are brainwashed with tales of a mighty and noble cause that they are fighting for. These upper echelon gang members sit in the S.H.U.'s, educate themselves, and come up with countless ways to utilize the troops that they have under them. Those with lower status do their bidding and get a smaller portion of the loot and it trickles down to the foot soldiers that get nothing but a pat on the back and some misguided feeling of pride. All for the cause! Believe it or not . . . this is a reality. I know from personal experience . . . I lived it from the time of impressionable adolescence to the criminally hard core violence and sophistication of La Nuestra Raza Prison Gang. False ideologies are continually being espoused within the gang structure. They are pounded into every soldier so that it always stays at the top of his priorities. This is done to keep the soldiers in line with the leaders' agenda and pumped up, ready for action. They speak of freedom of oppression from opposing gangs, yet the severely oppress their own.

Gangsters utilize a youngster's need for attention and acceptance against them. The words of praise are empty echoes intended to manipulate those who are being lauded. Words such as love, loyalty, and unity are used in an effort to trap new recruits and the common soldier into a sense of devotion. The words honor and duty are simply words of inspiration without substance used to induce those being fed the lies to act in accordance with the group's desires and objectives. They tell their members that the sacrifice of the few is for the common good of the many, when in fact, it is the other way around. Countless members sacrifice their freedom, their loved ones, and their lives for the good of the few who are in control.

All these things come into play in the recruitment and indoctrination of new recruits, the influence of all soldiers, and entrapment into the gang. I say entrapment because of the common "blood in, blood out" policy of most sophisticated and highly structured gangs. Once you are in the gang, you must participate in accordance with their agenda, or you are targeted for removal and/or assassination. This is the brutal truth about being a gang member. Make no bones about it.

"Gang Initiation - Blood In, Blood Out . . . a gang initiation - where to become a member, the person is jumped/ beat up by other members. I've heard that the only way out of some violent street gangs is impossible. Often, the method of departure is the same as one enters. Often there is no escape - it is an imprisonment of mind, body, and soul with socioeconomic ties and peer pressure interwoven in the fabric of the gangs." http://www.flickr.com

Blood in, Blood out!

Blood in . . . blood out!
It's the way of thugs . . .
Without a doubt.
Not kisses and hugs . . .
©©©
Just death and destruction.
Hatred and greed . . .
Their only function.
To make you bleed . . .
©©©
At the drop of a hat.
Kill you fast . . .
Just like that!
There ain't no pass . . .
©©©
Not in this game.
If you think there is . . .
You're really a lame.
So don't mess with this . . .
©©©
Only losers do.
Come in here . . .
And you'll be through!
Blood in . . . blood out!
©©©

All of this because our young ones blindly choose to accept the temporary and insidious adulation and false respect bestowed upon them by those with an agenda, who use it for their own selfish greed. Had our youngsters possessed the knowledge and enlightenment to develop the needed tools to make informed decisions, things might have been much different for them.

Gang involvement is not a worthy endeavor by any means, and woe to those who have to find this out the hard way. They have to learn the hard way and suffer the consequences and the pain of loneliness, despair, and heartbreak. It's a sad and lonely road that one travels as a gangster. Take my word for it . . . I've been there . . . all of my life. And not one single time in all of those years from neighborhood homie, to Norteno gang member, to being a member of influence in La Nuestra Raza prison gang, has a so called "brother" ever looked out for me or sent me money, stamps, or even a letter (other than business correspondence). That was left to your family to do, even though you still had to produce for the upper gang hierarchy. Just the way it was with us and just the way it is with most gangs.

But even so, after all of that, I continued to actively participate in gang behavior. Why? Because I had been instilled (through mental manipulation) with the attitudes and beliefs that I was a Norteno Warrior who was fighting for a valiant cause, regardless of the sacrifices I had to make. That cause being the war against oppression of my fellow and future Nortenos within the California Prison System (yeah right!) by the rival Mexican Mafia Prison Gang and their subordinate Surenos prison disruptive group. For some insane and incomprehensible reason or another, this belief gave me a false sense of pride and belonging that simply overrode my common sense and what little vestiges of decency that I still held on to. I believed I was a part of an honorable, important, and mighty struggle. I sure got one pulled over on me didn't I?

So much so, that I would knowingly step into an Administrative Segregation Yard controlled by the rival Surenos gang and rival White Aryan gang (a prison ally of the Surenos due to the alliance between the Mexican Mafia and the Aryan Brotherhood). I did so out of sheer stupidity and a false sense of bravado, but mostly because under the mandates of La Nuestra Raza (XIV Bonds), not to do so would be considered an act of cowardice by my peers, and would be just cause (in their eyes) to deem me as "no good" and target me for removal by physical attack.

CHAPTER TWELVE

Let's talk about drugs

Criminality, gangs, and drug activity only function as a result of our personal refusal to step up to the game and step up to the plate as individuals. We have a tendency to turn our backs on the issue as long as it doesn't involve us directly. In essence we tend to stick our heads in the proverbial sand, hoping that avoidance and ignorance will make the problems go away, or shield us from any adverse effects from these social issues. And that is exactly what they are . . . social issues. Therefore we, as a society, need to deal with them accordingly. We need to set boundaries early on to instill the proper ethics needed that will bring about a positive change in the attitudes and behaviors of our nation's children.

Let's take drugs for example. The United States of America is the number one consumer of illicit narcotics in the world. Many drug cartels in other countries have made fortunes off of the American appetite for Cocaine, Heroin, and other illicit narcotics. But once again we go back to the media where drug use is flaunted and seen as socially acceptable. Humanity has given it's very soul to the drug trade, the money it brings, and the power or at least sense of it that comes with drug trafficking. Drugs and our permissive acceptance of them are one of the very reasons that gangs exist in America. Drugs are their stock in trade. Without the black market need for illicit narcotics many gangs would just wither and die. Drug trafficking is a very lucrative business. So lucrative that as soon as one drug ring is busted up and put in jail by police, another one quickly takes its place. I know people who own $500,000.00 homes and drive expensive sports cars because of narcotics.

What is the relation between drugs and gangs?

Street gangs, outlaw motorcycle gangs (OMGs), and prison gangs are the primary distributors of illegal drugs on the streets of the United States. Gangs also smuggle drugs into the United States and produce and transport drugs within the country. Street gang members convert powdered cocaine into crack cocaine and produce most of the PCP available in the United States. Gangs, primarily OMGs, also produce marijuana and methamphetamine. In addition, gangs increasingly are involved in smuggling large quantities of cocaine and marijuana and lesser quantities of heroin, methamphetamine, and MDMA (also known as ecstasy) into the United States from foreign sources of supply. Gangs primarily transport and distribute powdered cocaine, crack cocaine, heroin, marijuana, methamphetamine, MDMA, and PCP in the United States.

Located throughout the country, street gangs vary in size, composition, and structure. Large, nationally affiliated street gangs pose the greatest threat because they smuggle, produce, transport, and distribute large quantities of illicit drugs throughout the country and are extremely violent. Local street gangs in rural, suburban, and urban areas pose a low but growing threat. Local street gangs transport and distribute drugs within very specific areas. These gangs often imitate the larger, more powerful national gangs in order to gain respect from rivals.

Some gangs collect millions of dollars per month selling illegal drugs, trafficking weapons, operating prostitution rings, and selling stolen property. Gangs launder proceeds by investing in real estate, recording studios, motorcycle shops, and construction companies. They also operate various cash-based businesses, such as barbershops, music stores, restaurants, catering services, tattoo parlors, and strip clubs, in order to commingle drug proceeds with funds generated through legitimate commerce.

What is the extent of gang operation and crime in the United States?

"There are at least 21,500 gangs and more than 731,000 active gang members in the United States. Gangs conduct criminal activity in all 50 states and U.S. territories. Although most gang activity is concentrated in major urban areas, gangs also are proliferating in rural and suburban areas of the country as gang members flee increasing law enforcement pressure in urban areas or seek more lucrative drug markets. This proliferation in nonurban areas increasingly is accompanied by violence and is threatening society in general."

"According to a 2001 Department of Justice survey, 20 percent of students aged 12 through 18 reported that street gangs had been present at their school during the previous 6 months. More than a quarter (28%) of students in urban schools reported a street gang presence, and 18 percent of students in suburban schools and 13 percent in rural schools reported the presence of street gangs. Public schools reported a much higher percentage of gang presence than private schools."

What are the dangers associated with gang activity?

"Large street gangs readily employ violence to control and expand drug distribution activities, targeting rival gangs and dealers who neglect or refuse to pay extortion fees. Members also use violence to ensure that members adhere to the gang's code of conduct or to prevent a member from leaving. In November 2004 a 19-year-old gang member in Fort Worth, Texas, was sentenced to 30 years in prison for fatally shooting a childhood friend who wanted to leave their local street gang."

"Authorities throughout the country report that gangs are responsible for most of the serious violent crime in the major cities

of the United States. Gangs engage in an array of criminal activities including assault, burglary, drive-by shooting, extortion, homicide, identification fraud, money laundering, prostitution operations, robbery, sale of stolen property, and weapons trafficking."

What are some signs that young people may be involved in gang activity?

"Changes in behavior such as skipping school, hanging out with different friends or, in certain places, spray-painting graffiti and using hand signals with friends can indicate gang affiliation."

"In addition, individuals who belong to gangs often dress alike by wearing clothing of the same color, wearing bandannas, or even rolling up their pant legs in a certain way. Some gang members wear certain designer labels to show their gang affiliation. Gang members often have tattoos. Also, because gang violence frequently is glorified in rap music, young people involved in gangs often try to imitate the dress and actions of rap artists."

"Finally, because substance abuse is often a characteristic of gang members, young people involved in gang activity may exhibit signs of drug or alcohol use."
http://www.justice.gov

Gangs see drugs and drug trafficking as an opportunity to have money and power, so they organize their little and big syndicates around the drug trade. Drugs . . . easily processed . . . easily transported . . . massively consumed . . . go figure! What else would gangs do?

The Impact of Drugs on Society

"The negative consequences of drug abuse affect not only individuals who abuse drugs but also their families and friends, various businesses, and government resources. Although many of these effects cannot be quantified, ONDCP recently reported that in 2002, the economic cost of drug abuse to the United States was $180.9 billion."

"The most obvious effects of drug abuse—which are manifested in the individuals who abuse drugs—include ill health, sickness and, ultimately, death. Particularly devastating to an abuser's health is the contraction of needle borne illnesses including hepatitis and HIV/AIDS through injection drug use. NSDUH data indicate that in 2004 over 3.5 million individuals aged 18 and older admitted to having injected an illicit drug during their lifetime. Of these individuals, 14 percent (498,000) were under the age of 25. Centers for Disease Control and Prevention (CDC) reports that 123,235 adults living with AIDS in the United States in 2003 contracted the disease from injection drug use, and the survival rate for those persons is less than that for persons who contract AIDS from any other mode of transmission. CDC further reports that more than 25,000 people died in 2003 from drug-induced effects."

"Children of individuals who abuse drugs often are abused or neglected as a result of the individuals' preoccupation with drugs. National-level studies have shown that parents who abuse drugs often put their need to obtain and abuse drugs before the health and welfare of their children. NSDUH data collected during 2002 and 2003 indicate that 4.3 percent of pregnant women aged 15 to 44 report having used illicit drugs in the past month. Moreover, that same data show that 8.5 percent of new mothers report having used illicit drugs in the past month. Children whose parents and other family members abuse drugs often are physically or emotionally abused and often lack proper immunizations, medical care, dental care, and necessities such as food, water, and shelter."

"The risk to children is even greater when their parents or guardians manufacture illicit drugs such as methamphetamine. Methamphetamine abusers often produce the drug in their own homes and apartments, using hazardous chemicals such as hydriodic acid, iodine, and anhydrous ammonia. Children who inhabit such homes often inhale dangerous chemical fumes and gases or ingest toxic chemicals or illicit drugs. These children commonly test positive for methamphetamine and suffer from both short- and long-term health consequences. Moreover, because many methamphetamine producers also abuse the drug, children commonly suffer from

neglect that leads to psychological and developmental problems. NCLSS data show that U.S. law enforcement agencies report having seized 9,895 illicit methamphetamine laboratories in 2004. These agencies report that 2,474 children were affected by these laboratories (i.e., they were exposed to chemicals, they resided at laboratory sites, or they were displaced from their homes), while 12 children were injured and 3 children were killed."

"The economic impact of drug abuse on businesses whose employees abuse drugs can be significant. While many drug abusers are unable to attain or hold full-time employment, those who do work put others at risk, particularly when employed in positions where even a minor degree of impairment could be catastrophic; airline pilots, air traffic controllers, train operators, and bus drivers are just a few examples. Quest Diagnostics, a nationwide firm that conducts employee drug tests for employers, reports that 5.7 percent of the drug tests they conducted on individuals involved in an employment-related accident in 2004 were positive. Economically, businesses often are affected because employees who abuse drugs sometimes steal cash or supplies, equipment, and products that can be sold to get money to buy drugs. Moreover, absenteeism, lost productivity, and increased use of medical and insurance benefits by employees who abuse drugs affect a business financially."

"The economic consequences of drug abuse severely burden federal, state, and local government resources and, ultimately, the taxpayer. This effect is most evident with methamphetamine. Clandestine methamphetamine laboratories jeopardize the safety of citizens and adversely affect the environment. Children, law enforcement personnel, emergency responders, and those who live at or near methamphetamine production sites have been seriously injured or killed as a result of methamphetamine production. Methamphetamine users often require extensive medical treatment; some abuse, neglect, and abandon their children, adding to social services costs; some also commit a host of other crimes including domestic violence, assault, burglary, and identity theft. Methamphetamine producer's tax strained law enforcement

resources and budgets as a result of the staggering costs associated with the remediation of laboratory sites. According to DEA, the average cost to clean up a methamphetamine production laboratory is $1,900. Given that an average of 9,777 methamphetamine laboratory seizures were reported to NCLSS each year between 2002 and 2004, the economic impact is obvious. DEA absorbs a significant portion of such costs through a Hazardous Waste Cleanup Program and in 2004 administered over 10,061 state and local clandestine laboratory cleanups and dumpsites at a cost of over $18.6 million. Nonetheless, resources of state and local agencies also are significantly affected. For example, 69 percent of the county officials responding to a 2005 survey by the National Association of Counties report that they had to develop additional training and special protocols for county welfare workers who work with children exposed to methamphetamine. Moreover, the time and manpower involved in investigating and cleaning up clandestine laboratories increase the workload of an already overburdened law enforcement system."
http://www.justice.gov

Top Ten Drugs and their effects

Drug abuse is a very common problem in most countries so it seemed like a good topic for a list. This is a list of ten of the most abused drugs and the effects they have on people.

1. Heroin

Heroin is an opiate processed directly from the extracts of the opium poppy. It was originally created to help cure people of addiction to morphine. Upon crossing the blood-brain barrier, which occurs soon after introduction of the drug into the bloodstream, heroin is converted into morphine, which mimics the action of endorphins, creating a sense of well-being; the characteristic euphoria has been described as an "orgasm" centered in the gut. One of the most common methods of heroin use is via intravenous injection.

2. Cocaine

Cocaine is a crystalline tropane alkaloid that is obtained from the leaves of the coca plant. It is both a stimulant of the central nervous system and an appetite suppressant, giving rise to what has been described as a euphoric sense of happiness and increased energy. It is most often used recreationally for this effect. Cocaine is a potent central nervous system stimulant. Its effects can last from 20 minutes to several hours, depending upon the dosage of cocaine taken, purity, and method of administration. The initial signs of stimulation are hyperactivity, restlessness, increased blood pressure, increased heart rate and euphoria. The euphoria is sometimes followed by feelings of discomfort and depression and a craving to experience the drug again. Sexual interest and pleasure can be amplified. Side effects can include twitching, paranoia, and impotence, which usually increases with frequent usage.
One of the best treatment for drug addiction is to consult with cocaine rehab centers for recovery.

3. Methamphetamine

Methamphetamine, popularly shortened to meth or ice, is a psychostimulant and sympathomimetic drug. Methamphetamine enters the brain and triggers a cascading release of norepinephrine, dopamine and serotonin. Since it stimulates the mesolimbic reward pathway, causing euphoria and excitement, it is prone to abuse and addiction. Users may become obsessed or perform repetitive tasks such as cleaning, hand-washing, or assembling and disassembling objects. Withdrawal is characterized by excessive sleeping, eating and depression-like symptoms, often accompanied by anxiety and drug-craving.

4. Crack Cocaine

Crack cocaine, often nicknamed "crack", is believed to have been created and made popular during the early 1980's. Because of the dangers for manufacturers of using ether to produce pure freebase cocaine, producers began to omit the step of removing the freebase precipitate from the ammonia mixture. Typically, filtration processes are also omitted. Baking soda is now most often used as a base rather than ammonia for reasons of lowered odor and toxicity; however, any weak base can be used to make crack cocaine. When commonly "cooked" the ratio is 1:1 to 2:3 parts cocaine/ bicarbonate.

5. LSD

Lysergic acid diethylamide, LSD, LSD-25, or acid, is a semisynthetic psychedelic drug of the tryptamine family. Arguably the most regarded of all psychedelics, it is considered mainly as a recreational drug, an entheogen, and a tool in use to supplement various types of exercises for transcendence including in meditation, psychonautics, and illegal psychedelic psychotherapy whether self-administered or not. LSD's psychological effects (colloquially called a "trip") vary greatly from person to person, depending on factors such as previous experiences, state of mind and environment, as well as dose strength. They also vary from one trip to another, and even as time passes during a single trip. An LSD trip can have long term psycho-emotional effects; some users cite the LSD experience as causing significant changes in their personality and life perspective. Widely different effects emerge based on what Leary called set and setting; the "set" being the general mindset of the user, and the "setting" being the physical and social environment in which the drug's effects are experienced.

6. Ecstasy

Ecstasy (MDMA) is a semisynthetic psychedelic entactogen of the phenethylamine family that is much less visual with more stimulant like effects than most all other common "trip" producing psychedelics. It is considered mainly a recreational drug that's often used with sex and associated with club drugs, as an entheogen, and a tool in use to supplement various types of practices for transcendence including in meditation, psychonautics, and illicit psychedelic psychotherapy whether self-administered or not. The primary effects of MDMA include an increased awareness of the senses, feelings of openness, euphoria, empathy, love, happiness, heightened self-awareness, feeling of mental clarity and an increased appreciation of music and movement. Tactile sensations are enhanced for some users, making physical contact with others more pleasurable. Other side effects, such as jaw clenching and elevated pulse, are common.

7. Opium

Opium is a resinous narcotic formed from the latex released by lacerating (or "scoring") the immature seed pods of opium poppies (Papaver somniferum). It contains up to 16% morphine, an opiate alkaloid, which is most frequently processed chemically to produce heroin for the illegal drug trade. Opium has gradually been superseded by a variety of purified, semi-synthetic, and synthetic opioids with progressively stronger effect, and by other general anesthesia. This process began in 1817, when Friedrich Wilhelm Adam Sertürner reported the isolation of pure morphine from opium after at least thirteen years of research and a nearly disastrous trial on himself and three boys.

8. Marijuana

Cannabis, known as marijuana in its herbal form, is a psychoactive product of the plant Cannabis sativa. Humans have been consuming cannabis since prehistory, although in the 20th century there was a rise in its use for recreational, religious or spiritual, and medicinal purposes. It is estimated that about four percent of the world's adult population use cannabis annually. It has psychoactive and physiological effects when consumed, usually by smoking or ingestion. The minimum amount of THC required to have a perceptible psychoactive effect is about 10 micrograms per kilogram of body weight. The state of intoxication due to cannabis consumption is colloquially known as a "high"; it is the state where mental and physical facilities are noticeably altered due to the consumption of cannabis. Each user experiences a different high, and the nature of it may vary upon factors such as potency, dose, and chemical composition, method of consumption and set and setting.

9. Psilocybin Mushrooms

Psilocybin mushrooms (also called psilocybin mushrooms) are fungi that contain the psychedelic substances psilocybin and psilocin, and occasionally other psychoactive tryptamines. There are multiple colloquial terms for psilocybin mushrooms, the most common being magic mushrooms or 'shrooms. When psilocybin is ingested, it is broken down to produce psilocin, which is responsible for the hallucinogenic effects. The intoxicating effects of psilocybin-containing mushrooms typically last anywhere from 3 to 7 hours depending on dosage, preparation method and personal metabolism. The experience is typically inwardly oriented, with strong visual and auditory components. Visions and revelations may be experienced, and the effect can range from exhilarating to distressing. There can be also a total absence of effects, even with large doses.

10. PCP

PCP (Phencyclidine) is a dissociative drug formerly used as an anesthetic agent, exhibiting hallucinogenic and neurotoxic effects. It is commonly known as Angel Dust, but is also known as Wet, Sherm, Sherman Hemsley, Rocket Fuel, Ashy Larry, Shermans Tank, Wack, Halk Hogan, Ozone, HannaH, Hog, Manitoba Shlimbo, and Embalming Fluid, among other names. Although the primary psychoactive effects of the drug only last hours, total elimination from the body is prolonged, typically extending over weeks. PCP is consumed in a recreational manner by drug users, mainly in the United States, where the demand is met by illegal production. It comes in both powder and liquid forms (PCP base dissolved most often in ether), but typically it is sprayed onto leafy material such as marijuana, mint, oregano, parsley or Ginger Leaves, and smoked. PCP has potent effects on the nervous system altering perceptual functions (hallucinations, delusional ideas, delirium or confused thinking), motor functions (unsteady gait, loss of coordination, and disrupted eye movement or nystagmus), and autonomic nervous system regulation (rapid heart rate, altered temperature regulation). The drug has been known to alter mood

states in an unpredictable fashion causing some individuals to become detached and others to become animated.
http://listverse.com/2007/09/27/top-10-drugs-and-their-effects

Straight Facts About Drugs and Alcohol Source:National Clearinghouse for Alcohol and Drug Information

"If your friend or loved one has one or more of the following signs, he or she may have a problem with drugs or alcohol:

- *Getting high on drugs or getting drunk on a regular basis*
- *Lying about things, or the amount of drugs or alcohol they are using*
- *Avoiding you and others in order to get high or drunk*
- *Giving up activities they used to do such as sports, homework, or hanging out with friends who don't use drugs or drink*
- *Having to use more marijuana or other illicit drugs to get the same effects*
- *Constantly talking about using drugs or drinking*
- *Believing that in order to have fun they need to drink or use marijuana or other drugs*
- *Pressuring others to use drugs or drink*
- *Getting into trouble with the law*
- *Taking risks, including sexual risks and driving under the influence of alcohol and/or drugs*
- *Feeling run-down, hopeless, depressed, or even suicidal*
- *Suspension from school for an alcohol- or drug-related incident*
- *Missing work or poor work performance because of drinking or drug use"*

"Many of the signs, such as sudden changes in mood, difficulty in getting along with others, poor job or school performance, irritability, and depression, might be explained by other causes.

Unless you observe drug use or excessive drinking, it can be hard to determine the cause of these problems. Your first step is to contact a qualified alcohol and drug professional in your area who can give you further advice."

"You may have a problem with drugs or alcohol, if

- *You can't predict whether or not you will use drugs or get drunk.*
- *You believe that in order to have fun you need to drink and/ or use drugs.*
- *You turn to alcohol and/or drugs after a confrontation or argument, or to relieve uncomfortable feelings.*
- *You drink more or use more drugs to get the same effect that you got with smaller amounts.*
- *You drink and/or use drugs alone.*
- *You remember how last night began, but not how it ended, so you're worried you may have a problem.*
- *You have trouble at work or in school because of your drinking or drug use.*
- *You make promises to yourself or others that you'll stop getting drunk or using drugs.*
- *You feel alone, scared, miserable, and depressed."*

"If you have experienced any of the above problems, take heart, help is available. More than a million Americans like you have taken charge of their lives and are living healthy and drug-free."

Messages for Teenagers

- *Know the law. Methamphetamines, marijuana, hallucinogens, crack, cocaine, and many other substances are illegal. Depending on where you are caught, you could face high fines and jail time. Alcohol is illegal to buy or possess if you are under 21.*

- *Be aware of the risks. Drinking or using drugs increases the risk of injury. Car crashes, falls, burns, drowning, and suicide are all linked to drug use.*
- *Keep your edge. Drug use can ruin your looks, make you depressed, and contribute to slipping grades.*
- *Play it safe. One incident of drug use could make you do something that you will regret for a lifetime.*
- *Do the smart thing. Using drugs puts your health, education, family ties, and social life at risk.*
- *Think twice about what you're advertising when you buy and wear T-shirts, hats, pins, or jewelry with a pot leaf, joint, blunt, beer can, or other drug paraphernalia on them. Do you want to promote something that can cause cancer? Make you forget things? or make it difficult to drive a car?*
- *Face your problems. Using drugs won't help you escape your problems, it will only create more.*
- *Be a real friend. If you know someone with a drug problem, be part of the solution. Urge your friend to get help.*
- *Remember, you DON'T NEED drugs or alcohol. If you think "everybody's doing it," you're wrong! Doing drugs won't make you happy or popular or help you to learn the skills you need as you grow up. In fact, doing drugs can cause you to fail at all of these things.*

How Can I Get Help?

"You can get help for yourself or for a friend or loved ones from numerous national, State, and local organizations, treatment centers, referral centers, and hotlines throughout the country. There are various kinds of treatment services and centers. For example, some may involve outpatient counseling, while others may be 3- to 5-week-long inpatient programs."

"While you or your friend or loved one may be hesitant to seek help, know that treatment programs offer organized and structured services with individual, group, and family therapy for people

with alcohol and drug abuse problems. Research shows that when appropriate treatment is given, and when clients follow their prescribed program, treatment can work. By reducing alcohol and/ or drug abuse, treatment reduces costs to society in terms of medical care, law enforcement, and crime. More importantly, treatment can help keep you and your loved ones together."

"Each community has its own resources. Some common referral sources that are often listed in the phone book are:
- *Community Drug Hotlines*
- *Local Emergency Health Clinics, or Community Treatment Services*
- *City/Local Health Departments*
- *Alcoholics Anonymous, Narcotics Anonymous, or Al-Anon/ Alateen*
- *Hospitals"*

http://www.athealth.com/Consumer/disorders/Substanceabuse. html

CHAPTER THIRTEEN

Conclusion

With that said I must warn all those who are at risk, or know someone who is at risk . . . to beware . . . before it's too late. It is my hope that the information and insight contained in these pages will help even one person to steer clear of, or be steered clear of the magnetic pull of the gangster lifestyle. Understandably most youth and street gang activity is not on the level of that which I have just described. But the warning is that absent any proper guidance, one can easily be drawn into the more serious and deadly levels of gang activity. It's not that far of a jump. It is a fact that most gang members find themselves in over their heads and just continue to spiral downward. It isn't a thought out plan, for most, but never the less they find themselves headed in that direction. It happens and it happens a lot . . . believe that!

I, among others, never had any intentions of becoming a member of La Nuestra Raza. It just followed as I continued into the lifestyle. I was ripe for recruitment and the recruiters were game tight. Recruiters to the more serious gangs are taught to be game tight. They can make joining their clique sound inviting, intriguing, and an honorable cause, and just. These guys spend years educating themselves on manipulation techniques in order to be good at what they do. They are experts in the wily ways of ruse, fraud, and deception. They will play a youngster like a well-tuned fiddle. They are taught to use words that lead and inspire, to get one to do their bidding, to work on a youngster's pride and incite their anger. They motivate and stir up emotions, because it is a known fact that an emotional person does not have his wits about him and can be easily drawn in. Young impressionable minds don't stand a chance against a well-seasoned gangster in the act of recruiting.

They make it sound really good . . . believe me. But it's all propaganda, and its force fed to the masses of recruits and soldiers alike. There is no future for gangsters . . . no security . . . no rainbow. It's simply pure unadulterated violence, greed, and hatred. Its hell in a hand basket and its set up to fail. You can't win. Nobody can. Everybody loses! Gangs do not work. They eventually all fail. Everyone involved is a casualty, from the specific ones to casualties in the broader sense. Its total anarchy and treachery.

It may look good, or promising, or exciting on television or in rap lyrics, but that is only staged fantasy. No one sees the ugly underbelly of the gangster lifestyle unless one is living in it. And by then my brother . . . it's already too late! There isn't any glamour, fame, or fortune in being a thug. Only prisons, death, and destruction. Movie stars like Al Pacino and rap stars like Spice One make their money by acting out thug roles and spouting thug lines and lyrics. But they are not real. It's all fantasy and it's what they do for a living. They sell you a dream. Their money doesn't come from real thuggin'. That's a persona they make up and sell to their audiences. It's Hollywood and the music industry who glamourize thuggin' and the millions who buy into the dream that makes being a gangster something exciting. But real gangsters and thugs end up in prison or dead. It's the way that it is. It's that simple.

©©©

You run around Raggin' . . .
Strollin' and Saggin"
Yeah you're real cool . . .
Silly young fool.
©©©
You're always in the mix . . .
But wait till you're in a fix.
Cause it ain't really cool . . .
That you're acting a fool.
©©©

It all leads to trouble . . .
When the law bursts your bubble.
And puts you in jail . . .
That's where your homies will fail . . .
©©©
To come around anymore.
And you'll know that for sure . . .
As you sit in your cell . . .
Without any mail.
©©©
But once you're cut loose . . .
It'll surely amuse,
To see them come round . . .
Cause the homie's in town!
©©©

Hanging with the homies, drinking, smoking weed, and flagging colors is easy to do because most kids in your neighborhood are doing the same thing. It's quick and easy acceptance with no judgments. I wanted that for myself, so that's what I did. It wasn't the right choice, not by a long shot. But I didn't have the knowledge or tools to know that. It was the easy choice and I took it, just as so many others do. But the trend needs to stop and it needs to stop where it all starts. At the young age of impressionable adolescence. That's where the brainwashing begins.

Do I blame the hood? Not anymore. Do I blame my circumstances? No, I'm the one who allowed my circumstances to mold me into the man I had become. Do I blame my neighborhood peers? Hardly, they were just as lost and confused as I was. Should I blame any of these things? With what I now know, I would say that the only one to blame was myself. The choices I made were mine alone to make. I was a pretty smart kid (scholastically) and could have been the exception had I chosen to do so.

But life goes on in the hood. It's relentless and unforgiving . . . but one can survive one's circumstances . . . or one can give in to them. One can play the game and be a hood hound . . . a rising star in the hood . . . catching all the ladies . . . driving a fancy car . . . and slinging dope for the homies. Or one can reach for the stars through education and awareness, attaining life skills. One can go to prison and even elevate one's gang status . . . get a life sentence or even wind up on a slab at the Coroner's Office. Or one can go to college . . . develop a career . . . and have a family of their own . . . and live life on one's own terms. Yes . . . life goes on in the hood. It doesn't stop for anyone, but anyone can make it stop. So get off of the merry-go-round of poverty, crime, and gangs. Choose instead, to excel in life . . . choose instead, to be somebody to someone . . . choose living!

Hoods are not that important. It's just a place where you live . . . nothing more. Get past it. Don't be like the rest who tattoo their hoods on their chests, their backs, their bellies, even their faces. For what? Is it a challenge? Who and what are they challenging? Why? Is it misplaced pride? Who cares? Only other thugs, and their opinions don't matter. At least they shouldn't, unless you're a thug too. State prisons are full of people like that. Society's failures who think that they have all the answers. I don't think so . . . they're in . . . or have been in . . . or will be in prison. What do they know? Does it really matter? No, not really. They are waiting to go back to the hood and do what they do, so that they can go back to prison. You do you . . . don't let them do you. That's how it's done.

The street game and gang-banging is built to fail. It's on full tilt . . . game over. No one shoots straight because everyone is trying to get over on each other. So failure is inevitable. And law enforcement is waiting on the sidelines with the Three Strikes Law, gang enhancements of various sorts, gang injunctions, gang validations, and various other law enforcement tools. They always get the thugs. They do it every single day. So failure comes at an ever increasing price. The million dollar question is: Are you willing to pay that price? I paid the price and I can tell you that I certainly did not like it. So just get it right. Gangster don't, they are in and out of prison most of their lives and many go back for the rest of their lives. Law enforcement is not playing around with these guys. I know 20 year olds who are doing 30 years or more their first time around.

11 Facts about Gangs

1. *Today's gangs are very sophisticated, crossing state lines to establish groups and recruit members as young as 10 years old in communities across the country.*

2. *Gangs use children because they know that whatever the child under thirteen does, he or she cannot go to jail.*

3. *32.4% of all the nation's cities, suburban towns and rural areas experienced gang problems in 2008.*

4. *To gang members, graffiti is a marking of territorial boundaries and serves as a warning or challenge to a rival gang.*

5. *Many kids join gangs because they do not receive adequate family attention, the gang provides love, identity and status; in turn they develop loyalty to the gang.*

6. *Many different ethnic, racial and socioeconomic groups make up gangs.*

7. *A number of well-known, wide-spread gangs such as the Crips, the Bloods and 18th Street originated in LA.*

8. *Gangs remain the primary distributors of drugs throughout the U.S.*

9. *Gangs are associating with organized crime entities, such as Mexican drug organizations, Asian criminal groups and Russian organized crime groups.*

10. *The Department of Justice estimates there are approximately 27,900 gangs, with 774,000 members, impacting communities across the United States.*

11. *Incarceration of gang members often does little to disrupt their activities, since high-ranking gang members are often able to exert their power on the street from within prison.*

http://www.dosomething.org/tipsandtools/11-facts-about-gangs

These are the cold hard facts about gangs. They are statistics that have been researched and proven many times over. Gangs are an epidemic across our land. They are powerful and exert an enormous amount of pressure on our young children as well as continue to affect our communities in negative ways. We are under siege by gangs of all types and ethnicities and they are growing bigger and stronger every day. They take hold of our youth and give them ersatz love and acceptance, so that they may influence and utilize them.

Prison doesn't stop the spread and growth of gangs. It only gives them more sophistication in the way they operate, and gives them much wider influence. When they come out of prison (if they come out) they are wiser to the ways of criminality, more dangerous, and more powerful. We all have idealistic views about how our world is supposed to be, but sans any effort or action on our part, there exists a darkness within our society with all its evil and criminality, where kidnappings, sex crimes, violence, crimes against children, gangs, drugs, murders, and psychopaths thrive openly and without regard for anyone's lives. Instead we should be experiencing love and decency with a sense of purpose and hope. Not a sinned stained world, torn and disfigured, marred by human incompetence. A testimony to man's futile and unsuccessful attempts at bringing about peace and harmony. Man's indifference has placed a tombstone on the grave of humanity and we are slowly filling in that dark hole. We must awaken ourselves to the knowledge that the privilege and responsibility of humanity belongs to us and that we would be wise to invest fully in that calling.

Self-Esteem Issues

Poor parental efforts and deep-seated social permissiveness bear the responsibility for the pervasive and unprecedented sense of low self-esteem in young adolescents today. From this comes an overwhelming yearning for acceptance of any kind. This opens the door for may gangs to thrive. Acceptance by any one person or group regardless of their moral stance, has emerged, and will continue to thrive absent any effort on our part. Our kids are simply grasping at straws, trying to replace the loss of the family as a cohesive, loving, and supportive unit. The lack of familial trust and love leaves gaping holes in a child's psyche that they will eventually struggle to fill, by anyone who embraces them. And as a result, most of them will find their way into a situation that, more often than not, will lead them right into the waiting arms of gangster thugs. These thugs know that youngsters' minds are ripe for exploitation and they take full advantage of that.

A big responsibility of parents is to bring up their children. There are many issues you need to take care of while your children go through the various stages of their childhood. Self-esteem in children is one such thing that needs to be given attention and importance.

Self-esteem is not a quality that can be expressed in words. It is a quality which should be visible through your personality and behavior. Self-esteem means being comfortable with yourself and accepting the person inside you. You must be proud of the good within yourself and also be aware of the bad within you. It's all about liking yourself. Ever wonder how a person cannot like himself? Just think about some people you know; are they completely happy? They are not happy about some or the other aspect of themselves. Some are unhappy about their looks, some want more money, some want another job. Some wish to change their career path, while some are unhappy with their family relationships. These people have low self-esteem. What about self-esteem in children? You as a parent should remember the above things and take care that you nurture your child in the right way. It is your responsibility that he/she does not end up being one in a crowd of children with self-esteem issues.

A child having self-esteem is creative, happy, active, and has more confidence. What parent wouldn't like to watch their children to be like this? Children derive confidence about themselves from the way they are treated, mostly by their parents. You play the important role of giving them a sense of self-worth.

Building Self Esteem in Children

Love your Children for Who They Are

"Always trying to point out mistakes in your children will make them feel very low. Remember to encourage them for their smallest achievements. Stop blaming them unnecessarily, thinking that this will make them more perfect. As you point out their mistakes, get into the habit of pointing out their good qualities as well. Everyone has some minus points; help your children to overcome those. Try to find the best in them and also make them realize about their plus points. Don't blame them if they lack some qualities. Instead try to enhance the qualities they possess."

Give them Solutions: Show the Right Way
"You definitely need to point out the mistakes to your children, but in a proper manner. Point out their mistakes and tell them the reason behind calling it a 'mistake'. Many a times, things that are wrong according to you would be perfectly right according to your children. Tell them the right way. Also, encourage them to perform the same activity again, it's like giving them another chance and hence, showing the confidence that they will do it right this time."

Do Not Compare
"As you hate comparisons, so do your children. Many a times, people compare their children with his/her classmates, neighbors or buddies in terms of exam grades, homework completion, general habits, etc. Mind well, that this is the most dangerous thing you are doing to your child. Though young, he/she will understand that this is wrong and feel the un-satisfactoriness within you towards them."

Give Importance to School but Don't Make a Hype
"Many parents and teachers believe that school is the only thing in the life of a child. Stop making hype of their homework and exams. Many times children end up doing the homework just for the sake of completing it. Tell them the importance of homework and the right way to complete it in time. Let them decide the time for their studies. Don't force a schedule over them that are made by you. This will hamper the child's development."

Give them Importance
"Always saying, 'what do you know, you are young' is unhealthy for your children. Listen to them, learn to understand them and give them enough of your time. Respect their likes and dislikes as you expect them to respect yours. You can ask for their opinion in some things related or not related to them. This will make them

feel that they are a part of the family and their views and choices are given importance and value."

Take the Pressure Off

"Your children may be under pressure due to many reasons like exams, illness, performance, fights with buddies, etc. Try to take off their pressure by discussing the issue with them. Talk to them and make them feel comfortable and relaxed so that they feel secured to share their problems with you."

"Indulge your children in some group activities. Games, scouting, dancing are some activities for children with low self-esteem. But, consider the likes and interests of your children and accordingly decide the activity for them. Understanding your children well is a primary responsibility for building self-esteem in children."

By Mamta Mule
http://www.buzzle.com/articles/self-esteem-in-children

Lack of these factors make for easy manipulation and assimilation into the gang culture, where seemingly undying unity and love, as well as belonging and acceptance are erroneously the order of the day. We need to pay attention and take notice. We must respond with an open heart, an open mind, and very open ears. An investment in our children is always an investment in our future.

Gangster life callin', thuggin' and ballin' is only a dream, but it is a dream well sold to the nation's youth. Don't get it twisted though, youngsters buy it lock, stock, and barrel, and are more and more willing to sacrifice themselves for the sake of the gang. But it's set to fail because it's built on a false pretext. It's temporary at best. At least your child's involvement in it is. The gangs and drugs go on . . . right to the next victim. Yes . . . it's fatal to most that enter into it.

They sell it in the beats . . . they sell it in the videos . . . and they sell it in the movies. But what they sell in the media is all fantasy, yet it draws our youth to the real deal. Movies and Music glorify the death of a thug, when in reality; there is nothing honorable about dying as a criminal.

Take the death of Tupac Shakur for example. For all his money and fame, he died in a hail of bullets because he tried to play the gangster role in his life. He was persistent in perpeturating the East Coast/West Coast rivalry and because of that he got everyday thugs involved in his drama. When you put your chest out there and create a challenge someone will always be around to answer the call. Although he was a famous rapper, he lived the life of a thug and that lifestyle brought reality right to his doorstep in the form of assassins' bullets.

The death of Tupac Shakur in Las Vegas

Frank Wilkins

Timeline of Events
8:39pm: *Mike Tyson knocks out Bruce Seldon at the MGM Grand Hotel, in Las Vegas*

8:45pm: *As Tupac Shakur leaves the MGM Grand, he gets into an altercation with a young black man believed to be Orlando Anderson, member of a rival gang, The Southside Crips. MGM security video catches the incident on tape.*

The fight is stopped by security. A man involved in the fight with Shakur is held for questioning and then let go. The police never got the man's name.

8:55pm: *The Death Row entourage leaves the MGM Grand and stops by the Luxor Hotel on the Las Vegas Strip for reasons not known, then proceeds to Suge Knight's house southeast of downtown.*

Time Unknown: *The 10-car Death Row entourage leaves the mansion en route to Knight's Club 662, located about 10 blocks east of the Las Vegas Strip at 1700 E. Flamingo Road. Tupac Shakur and Knight ride in his black BMW 750.*

Approx. 10:55pm: *Tupac Shakur rolls down the passenger side window to allow someone to take the above photo at a red light.*

Approx. 11:10pm: The BMW is stopped by bicycle police on the Las Vegas strip for not having a license plate on the car (the plates are in the trunk) and for playing music too loud. No ticket is issued.

Approx. 11:15pm: On Flamingo Road, near the intersection of Koval Lane, a white 4-door Cadillac with California plates rolls up to the passenger side of the BMW. According to one witness, two men got out of the Cadillac and fire 13 rounds from a Glock .40 calibre handgun at the BMW from less than 13 feet away. Tupac Shakur, sitting in the passenger side of the car, is hit three times, one striking his hip, another his right hand, with the fatal wound to his chest. According to the witness, Tupac Shakur attempts to jump into the back seat of the car as he is being shot but Suge pulls him down into the seat. Two tires are punctured in the barrage of gunfire. Knight suffers a minor wound to his head or neck. Suge turns to Tupac and asks "Are you OK Pac?" Tupac Shakur, after seeing blood on Knight's head says, "Me? You're the one shot in the mutha-fuckin' head!"

11:16pm: Knight makes a U-turn on Flamingo, races west to Las Vegas Boulevard, makes a left turn. After encountering heavy traffic on the strip Knight's car hits the median blowing out a third tire and comes to a stop near the intersection of Harmon Avenue.

11:16 - 11:20pm: Up to 20 police officers arrive at the scene

Approx. 11:30pm: An ambulance arrives and whisks Tupac Shakur and Knight to University Medical Center. As Tupac is being removed from the vehicle he repeats, "I can't breathe, I can't breathe."

September 13, 1996; 4:03pm: Tupac Shakur dies from his wounds six days after being placed into a medically induced coma.

The Witnesses
One of Tupac Shakur's backup rappers who witnessed the fatal shooting of the hip-hop star was gunned down in a New Jersey housing project days after Tupac was shot. So far, police are saying that the slaying of 19-year-old Yafeu Fula has no connection with Tupac's death

But Fula's death will further stymie the slow-moving murder investigation. "It's another dead end for us," said Las Vegas police Sgt. Kevin Manning, the lead investigator.

Police found Fula at 3:48 a.m. Sunday in a housing project. He was shot once in the head and was pronounced dead later that afternoon at a nearby hospital.

Two suspects, both juveniles, were arrested and are being questioned by Orange police. "As far as we know, at this time, there is no connection" to Shakur, said Capt. Richard Conte

Fula, a member of Tupac Shakur's backing group Outlaw Immortalz, was riding with bodyguards in the car behind Shakur when the rapper was shot by unknown assailants returning from the Tyson-Bruce fight September 7 in Las Vegas. Police questioned Fula after the drive-by, but, like others in the Death Row Records entourage, he subsequently refused to cooperate with police.

The one bright spot in an otherwise dire news week at Death Row came courtesy of Shakur's posthumous album, The Don Killuminati—The 7 Day Theory. Recorded under the alias Makaveli, the collection entered the charts at No. 1, with incredibly strong sales of 664,000 copies.

CASE UPDATE: Based on new evidence - which has not been made public - a task force consisting of local Los Angeles and national law enforcement officials has recently begun re-investigating the murder of rap artist Christopher Wallace (a.k.a. Biggie, Biggie Smalls, Notorious B.I.G.) more than a decade after he was gunned down on the streets in Los Angeles.

Biggie, from the Bedford-Stuyvesant area of Brooklyn took 4 bullets to the chest as he was leaving a Soul Train Awards after-party. He was later pronounced dead after not responding to treatment at L.A.'s Cedars-Sinai Hospital.

In the 13 years since his death, there have been many rumors speculating on the identity and motive of Biggie's killer, with the most widely accepting being that the shooting was retaliation for the murder of Death Row Records rapper Tupac Shakur who was shot in 1996 on the streets of Las Vegas. Former LAPD detective Russell Poole, who was involved in the 1997 investigation, maintains the belief that Wallace's murder was ordered by Death Row Records' co-founder and former CEO, Marion "Suge" Knight. "Suge Knight ordered the hit," says Poole, alleging that David Mack, a former LAPD officer, was the one who fired the fatal shots.

Despite the long running imbroglio between Wallace and Tupac during the height of the East Coast-West Coast feud, the rappers' mothers, Voletta Wallace and Afeni Shakur, have denounced the culture of violence that took their sons. The couple joined voices to speak out against violence during a memorable MTV Video Awards presentation back in 1999.

Voletta Wallace told AllHipHop, "All I want, all I ever wanted, is justice for my son's death. All I ever wanted was the truth. And that's not asking too much."

Stay tuned as we're likely to hear more on the results of the investigation in the coming months. Might the actual killers of both artists be revealed once the investigation is over?

http://www.franksreelreviews.com/shorttakes/tupac.htm

Another rapper who tried to live his life as a thug and a gangster was the Notorious B.I.G. Christopher Wallace. He also died in a hail of bullets. When rappers confuse what they do for a living with the cold hard reality of gangs, they usually reap what they sow.

A Time Line Of Notorious B.I.G's Life After Death

Written by jazzyf on March 9, 2011 12:00 pm

Christopher Wallace born May 21st 1972 went by many names; Biggie Smalls, Frank White, The Notorious B.I.G., but he obtained the title King of New York when he died March 9th 1997. The Notorious B.I.G. is one of few hip-hop artists whose legacy may live on forever. Biggie Smalls was "Black and ugly as ever" by his own admission but was considered by most to be very charming, especially with the ladies. The Brooklyn born MC was first heard by the world on Mary J. Blige's "Real Love" remix and later released his debut album Ready to Die in 1994. Thanks to hits like the celebratory "Juicy" the hip-hop community immediately fell in love with Biggie. It did not take long for the record to go platinum, and the Notorious B.I.G. was named MC of the Year at the 1995 Billboard Music Awards.

WBW: Top 9 Music Videos Of The 2000s

The Notorious B.I.G.'s rise to fame was not easy. As he would put it, he went from "Ashy to Classy" overnight. Coming from the streets of Bedford Stuyvesant, Brooklyn, he lived a life of crime. Biggie dropped out of high school at the age of 17 to become a crack dealer. A routine trip to North Carolina for a drug exchange landed him in jail for nine months. Once released Christopher Wallace began recording rhymes with Mister Cee a well-known New York City radio DJ. "Sean Puffy Combs" at the time still working at Uptown records heard Biggie's early recordings and was impressed. Leaving Uptown to start his own label Bad Boy Entertainment, Diddy decided to sign Biggie to the label and the frenzy began from there.

Top 9 Music Videos Of The 1990s

Along with his successful career Christopher Wallace was responsible for bringing his crew Junior Mafia to fame. Lil Kim the first lady of the group would go on to become a rap icon and to some, Hip Hip's rap queen.

Things took a turn for the worst on November 30, 1994. The day before he was due in court for a sexual assault charge Tupac Shakur was shot five times and robbed after entering the lobby of Quad Recording Studios in Manhattan by two armed men. Pac was shot in the head, groin, leg and thigh and accused Biggie, Puffy and Andre Harrell—who were there recording the same night—of setting him up.

The next day, Tupac Shakur showed up to the courthouse in a wheelchair and was found guilty of three counts of molestation. February 6, 1995, he was sentenced to one and a half to four and a half years in prison on a sexual assault charge. While incarcerated he released the multi-platinum "Me Against The World" which would sell 240,000 copies in the first week and remain at the top of Billboard charts for five weeks. Later Tupac signed with CEO of Death Row Records Suge Knight. The deal was made due to a $1.4 million bail made by Suge Knight pending appeal of the conviction in exchange for Shakur to release three albums under the Death Row label, the feud would only get worse from this point on.

Tupac was shot on September 7, 1996 in Las Vegas and died several days later from cardiac arrest. Six months after that Biggie was killed in Los Angeles.

After fourteen years the details have been regrettably forgotten by some, so TheUrbanDaily.com decided to compile a list of information that has occurred since the death of The Notorious B.I.G.

1997
In February The Notorious BIG traveled out to Los Angeles, California to promote his upcoming album Life After Death, scheduled to be release March 25th. BIG and Sean "Puffy" Combs shot the music video for the first single "Hypnotize" as well.

March 5th Biggie did a radio interview with The Dog House on KYLD in San Francisco, California where he spoke about hiring security because he feared for his safety.

March 8th- *Biggie presented an award at The Soul Train Music Awards where he was booed by some of the crowd. Afterward Biggie attended the after party at Petersen Automotive Museum in Los Angeles hosted by Vibe Magazine and Qwest records. Several celebrity guests were in attendance. The party was shut down by the fire department due to overcrowding.*

March 9th - *At around 12:30 AM Biggie and his entourage left in two GMC Suburbans to return to his hotel, Wallace seated in the front passenger seat alongside Damion "D-Roc" Butler, Lil' Cease and driver, Gregory "G-Money" Young. Sean Combs traveled in the other vehicle with three bodyguards. Bad Boy's director of security followed the two trucks from behind in a Chevrolet Blazer. The streets were filled with people leaving the after party.*

Biggie's truck stopped at a red light near the museum when a black Chevrolet Impala pulled up alongside the vehicle. The driver of the Impala, an African American male dressed in a blue suit and bow tie, rolled down his window with a 9 mm blue-steel pistol in hand and fired at the vehicle. Four bullets hit Wallace in the chest. His entourage rushed him to Cedars-Sinai Medical Center, where he was pronounced dead at 1:15 a.m. Wallace's murder remains unsolved and there are many theories regarding the identities and motives of the murderers.

In 2002, Randall Sullivan released a book Labyrinth, compiling evidence by retired LAPD detective Russell Poole regarding the murders of Christopher Wallace and Tupac Shakur. Marion "Suge" Knight, co-founder of Death Row Records and allegedly Blood gang affiliated, was accused of conspiring with David Mack, an LAPD officer and alleged Death Row security employee, to murder Christopher Wallace to make his and Shakur's death appear to be the result of a bi-coastal rap rivalry. Sullivan believed Amir Muhammad, who also goes by the name Harry Billups and was an associate of Mack's, was the shooter based on evidence provided by an anonymous informant and his resemblance to the facial composite. An investigative documentary Biggie & Tupac by filmmaker Nick Broomfield was also released based on evidence from the book.

In March 2005, the relatives of Wallace filed a wrongful death claim against the LAPD based on the evidence compiled by Russell Poole. They claimed the LAPD had sufficient evidence to make an arrest, but never did. David Mack and Amir Muhammad (a.k.a. Harry Billups) were originally named as defendants in the civil suit, but were dropped before the trial began after the LAPD and FBI dismissed them as suspects.

July of 2005, the case was declared a mistrial after the judge was concerned that the police were withholding evidence. An attempt to expand the wrongful death lawsuit to include new claims failed in August 2006. The criminal investigation was re-opened in July 2006.

On January 19, 2007, Tyruss Himes aka Big Syke, a friend of Shakur who was implicated in the murder by television channel KTTV and XXL magazine in 2005, had a defamation lawsuit regarding the accusations thrown out of court.

On April 16, 2007, the family of Christopher Wallace filed a second wrongful death lawsuit against the city of Los Angeles. The suit also named two LAPD officers in the center of the investigation, Rafael Perez and Nino Durden. According to the claim, Perez, an alleged affiliate of Death Row Records, admitted to LAPD officials that he and Mack "conspired to murder, and participated in the murder of Christopher Wallace." The Wallace family said the LAPD "consciously concealed Rafael Perez's involvement in the murder of Christopher Wallace. A U.S. district judge dismissed the lawsuit on December 19, 2007.

Los Angeles Judge Florence-Marie Cooper reinstated the lawsuit on May 9, 2008. With the agreement of both sides, the lawsuit was dismissed April 5, 2010 without prejudice to re-filing.
A few weeks before the 2011 anniversary of Christopher Wallace's death new information has surfaced from Rafael Perez's cellmate, who claims Perez released info to him.

The original lead detective investigating Wallace's murder says Mack and Perez had close ties to Death Row.

Months after Biggie's murder, officers Mack and Perez were convicted for unrelated crimes—Mack for bank robbery, Perez for stealing cocaine and several other felony charges. According to court records that have been recently revealed, Perez's cell mate told investigators "Perez and Mack were involved with Death Row Records. Perez was involved with Death Row through Mack. They went to all their parties and events," the inmate stated.

Investigators say Perez also told the inmate he was at the scene of the Wallace murder. "Perez was working security. Perez had a cell phone. Perez said he called David Mack on his cell phone and told Mack that Biggie Smalls was in his truck. Perez never said that he set up Biggie Smalls but I have heard that he . . . had something to do with that murder," according to the inmate.

Former lead investigator Russell Poole, who resigned in 1999, says these statements are just a glimpse into hundreds of pages of documents that were hidden from Wallace family attorneys. He believes the murder of Christopher Wallace should be put into a historical context. Beginning with the Rodney King beating which occurred five years before and the criminal trial of O.J. Simpson in 1995.

Officer Perez was on duty the night of Christopher Wallace's murder and if his involvement is confirmed the city of Los Angeles could be liable for hundreds of millions of dollars in damages. Perez and Mack have repeatedly denied any involvement in the murder. http://theurbandaily.com/music

The real losers in this supposed battle between Tupac Shakur and the Notorious B.I.G. was not them. They are dead . . . they don't feel anything. The real losers were their mothers who suffered the loss of their sons and the attention of the world in their private lives. The heartache of watching their sons drift off into the world of gangs, guns, and drugs. To be eventually carried away by death. That's who lost! And that's the real deal.

Let me tell you what else is real. The loneliness and heartache from missing and being away from loved ones. I'm just saying though. One may act tough and put on a façade of bravado, but deep inside one feels the hurt and the loneliness . . . that's a fact. I've witnessed it from some seemingly tough gangsters during mail call in prison, as they wait to hear from those who love them. It doesn't feel so good when the mailman passes by your cell day after day without dropping something off to you. I've experienced it myself throughout the years. It is heart-wrenching even to the toughest of thugs.

And even when you do hear from your loved ones, just to read the sadness and strife that is evident between the lines and the loneliness that your actions have caused those that you love is sad. It is hard on families who are left to fend for themselves, or even worse, have to fend for themselves and for you.

Dealing with a family member in prison can be a challenge for those left behind, who may feel anger, grief, guilt, betrayal, overwhelmed and isolation from the community. Staying in touch with a family member in jail can be a heartbreaking and complicated thing. Not only is it difficult to keep in touch through unpredictable phone access and prison transfers; having a husband, wife, sibling, parent, child, friend, or other relative behind bars can be a devastating emotional experience. Your loved one can't help you through this—in fact, he or she may be part of the problem—so it's important to learn to give yourself the care and support you'll need throughout this trying time.

Keeping in touch, whether by in-person visits, phone calls or snail mail letters can be a double-edged sword. It's a virtual part-time job to figure out prison schedules and which day's visits are allowed; phone calls can only be made out of the prison, not in; and even sending letters can get complicated when a prisoner is moved unexpectedly. What's more, people change and relationships change when you're not able to interact naturally for an extended period of time—especially when something as loaded as crime and a prison sentence stand between you, but can't easily be discussed.

Then there is the stress of trying to survive gang life within the walls of prison and its politics and games. This is very taxing to an individual. Real gangs are a life threatening business where the price of a life comes very cheap. As a gangster you live and die by the proverbial gun. It is a cutthroat business and absent any morals what so ever. It's a jungle sometimes and it's hard to keep from going under. Gangsters have to fight and scratch their way through an unforgiving environment, where trust is not lightly given, even among brothers in the same cause. In fact I know that in the group I was a part of, any time you had to interact with people outside of the group, you had to have another member there to ensure your loyalty.

And individuals themselves do not trust easily. One's brothers in arms are many times the very ones that one has to look out for. And the ones closer to you are even harder to trust because those are the ones that will be sent to do you, should you be targeted for removal or assassination. They have access and opportunity and will without a doubt be used for that purpose should it be called for. They are the ones who will catch you slipping.

©©©
You got caught slipping . . .
Fool why you tripping?
You knew it would happen . . .
I bet you're not laughing.
©©©
It was your time to go . . .
Cause the cuetero said so.
The vato next to you . . .
Had to do his due.
©©©
You never saw it coming . . .
As he came up running.
Put a shank in you . . .
To let you know you're through.
©©©
You were marked from above . . .
By those who swore their love . . .
And loyalty to you . . .
Fool . . . I thought you knew.
©©©
That's the way it's played . . .
That's the bed that you made!

There simply isn't any excuse for the permissively rampant society that we live in today. Today, laws have been enacted and rules changed that encourage permissiveness and a lack of accountability. The rights or responsibility of a parent to raise his or her child has been somewhat diminished by the role of government, which can possibly punish the parent in some instances. Likewise school officials have been stripped of their ability to enforce discipline in unruly students. Everyone everywhere is scared to death that they will be arrested for some sort of abuse in dealing with their children or with their students too harshly. So much so, that they pretty much let them run around virtually unchecked.

Schools have become a killing zone and teachers are terrified of their charges. But who can say what discipline is too harsh? Who can draw the line and why? The bible counsels us to use discipline on our children and it does so for a reason. For the proper up-bringing of one's children. It is wise counsel and we as a society should enact laws that are in accordance with that scriptural wisdom.

Half a century back television sit-coms such as "I Love Lucy"; "Leave It To Beaver"; and "Mary Tyler Moore" adhered to a good moral standard and strict family values. They had twin beds in the bedroom, wore pajamas, and did not act out sexual encounters as a part of their programming, and they were highly successful sit-coms. They didn't have to "sell sex" or be provocative in nature to sell their show. They were just funny and entertaining. There was not any inappropriate behavior, foul language, or sexual misconduct.

Today's "prime time" television is all about sexual immorality, drugs, and violence. Women are dressing in sexually provocative attire, if any at all, behaving in a promiscuous manner, with foul language and moral ineptitude. And all of it seems to be socially acceptable. Our kids watch all this stuff on evening television, watch these and other even more provocative actions on the internet, and listen to violence, hatred, and disrespect of females in their rap music. Sex . . . sex . . . sex . . . that's all there is! And then we wonder why our children are the way they are. Unbelievable.

Everything that is advertised now days has the sexual connotation to it. It seem as if Americans are fixated with sex and sexual images and can only relate or react to that type of visual stimulation in buying things. Even women seem to respond to the sexist advertisements and are being targeted aggressively in the media.

They say the game is on tight! But don't you believe it. They just want you to bite. The lure of easy money, fast cars, and faster women is what they sell you on. It looks good in the movies . . . it sounds good in the videos . . . it even has a good beat. Flashing all that bling (gold and diamonds), making all that scrilla (money), smoking big fat blunts (marijuana rolled in cigar leaves), acting like they are above the law. Yeah Right! It's all pure propaganda made up to excite and incite young people to buy what they are selling.

Even the real gangsters got on the bandwagon with their own CDs called Generation of United Nortenos (G.U.N.) and Seventeen Reasons. It was one of the most skillfully masterminded recruiting tools of our time. Meant to excite, intrigue, and recruit Nortenos in unprecedented numbers . . . and it worked! The masterminds behind G.U.N. were none other than La Nuestra Familia Prison Gang. G.U.N. was such a success that the F.B.I. pulled it from store shelves and outlawed it.

It was a plot, a ruse, thought up by the ruling elite and carried out by a ranking Nuestra Familia member who was released form Pelican Bay and was given the funds to produce it. Because of this, La Nuestra Familia's rule flourished in Northern California through recruited regiments of Nuestra Raza soldiers under the command of a Nuestra Familia member. Drugs, murder, and mayhem ruled the day. Youngsters were pumped up, ready to do the Nuestra Familia's bidding by killing Surenos and Bulldogs (a drop-out faction of the Norteno Prison disruptive group, specifically from Fresno and surrounding Fresno County towns.), selling drugs, and committing countless crimes. They were ready to join the regiments, but to the Nuestra Familia they were simply a means to an end. The enrichment of the ruling elite!

They were a tool . . . nothing more. Used to achieve the Nuestra Familias leaders' personal agendas. This is a prime example of how gangs use the power and influence of the mass media to exploit youngsters. Think about that the next time you sit down with your child to watch a violent gangster film, or as you sit idly by while your child listens to some savage gangsta lyrics. Look around in your neighborhood and you'll see the signs of gangster life. Some young thug balling out of control. But look quick because he won't be there for very long. Not to worry though because there will be another to take his place. Maybe your child. Think about that.

They say the game is on tight . . .
but we've really lost sight . . .
Of the things that are real . . .
We can't even feel . . . .

Where has the love gone?
Where did we go wrong?
Its humanities curse . . .
and Society's hearse!

For the sake of the dollar . . .
We all scream and holler!
but is it worth it?
Look where we sit.

A world gone mad . . .
hinging on bad.
Souls that are lost . . .
boy what a cost!

We're living a lie . . .
Ready to die.
and nobody cares . . .
Is that really fair?
No, not really!!!

TV Bloodbath: Violence on Prime Time Broadcast TV
A PTC State of the Television Industry Report

I. Introduction

The Debate is Over

"Concerns about the impact of television violence on society are almost as old as the medium itself. As early as 1952, the United States House of Representatives was holding hearings to explore the impact of television violence and concluded that the "television broadcast industry was a perpetrator and a deliverer of violence." In 1972 the Surgeon General's office conducted an overview of existing studies on television violence and concluded that it was "a contributing factor to increases in violent crime and antisocial behavior." In his testimony to the U.S. Senate Subcommittee on Communications, Surgeon General Jesse Steinfeld said, "It is clear to me that the causal relationship between televised violence and antisocial behavior is sufficient to warrant appropriate and immediate remedial action . . . There comes a time when the data are sufficient to justify action. That time has come."

"Over the years, there have been literally hundreds of studies examining the connection between media violence and violence in real-life, the results of which were summarized in a joint statement signed by representatives from six of the nation's top public health organizations, including the American Academy of Pediatrics, the American Psychological Association, and the American Medical Association: "Well over 1000 studies . . . point overwhelmingly to a causal connection between media violence and aggressive behavior in some children. The conclusion of the public health community, based on over 30 years of research, is that viewing entertainment violence can lead to increases in aggressive attitudes, values and behavior, particularly in children."

"Today, the connection between media violence and aggressive and violent behavior in real life has been so well documented, that for many, the question is settled. In fact, a position paper by the American Psychiatric Association on media violence begins by declaring: "The debate is over." According to Jeffrey McIntyre, legislative and federal affairs officer for the American Psychological Association, "To argue against it is like arguing against gravity."

"Earlier this year at a Senate Commerce Committee hearing on neurobiological research and the impact of media on children, Dr. Michael Rich, Director of the Center on Media and Children's Health at the Children's Hospital of Boston testified that the correlation between violent media and aggressive behavior "is stronger than that of calcium intake and bone mass, lead ingestion and lower IQ, condom non-use and sexually acquired HIV, and environmental tobacco smoke and lung cancer, all associations that clinicians accept as fact, and on which preventive medicine is based without question."

The Impact of Media Violence

"Television can be profoundly influential in shaping an impressionable child or adolescent's values, attitudes, perceptions, and behaviors. Television reaches children at a younger age and for more time than any other socializing influence, except family. The average child spends 25 hours a week watching television, more time than they spend in school or engaged in any other activity except sleep. Is it any wonder then that children so readily absorb the messages that are presented to them?"

So what is the cumulative impact of 25 hours of television a week?

"It is estimated that by the time an average child leaves elementary school, he or she will have witnessed 8,000 murders and over 100,000 other acts of violence. By the time that child is 18 years-of-age; he or she will witness 200,000 acts of violence, including 40,000 murders. One 17-year longitudinal study concluded that teens who watched more than one hour

of TV a day were almost four times as likely as other teens to commit aggressive acts in adulthood."

"Television teaches viewers—especially young viewers, who have more difficulty discriminating between real life and fantasy—that violence is the accepted way we solve problems. Moreover, studies show that the more real-life the violence portrayed, the greater the likelihood that it will be learned."

"And while it's true that not every child who is exposed to a lot of televised violence is going to grow up to be violent, "every exposure to violence increases the chances that someday a child will behave more violently than they otherwise would," according to Dr. L. Rowell Huesmann of the University of Michigan."

"Violent entertainment leaves a mark, even on children who don't engage in aggressive behaviors. Witnessing repeated violent acts increases general feelings of hostility and can lead to desensitization and a lack of empathy for human suffering. Over time, consumption of violence-laden imagery can leave viewers with the perception that they are living in a mean and dangerous world, giving them an unrealistically dark view of life."

"For children who do act out aggressively, the results can be deadly. Week after week, newspapers are filled with blood-chilling accounts of children committing copy-cat crimes inspired by the latest horror film or violent video game."

The Slippery Slope of TV Violence

"Entertainment violence is a slippery slope. With repeated exposure, even the most gruesome and grisly depictions of violence eventually seem tame. In time, viewers become desensitized, so Hollywood has to keep pushing the envelope in order to elicit the same reaction."

"Lt. Col. David Grossman, author of Stop Teaching Our Kids to Kill, explains: "Violence is like the nicotine in cigarettes. The reason why the media has to pump ever more violence into us is

because we've built up a tolerance. In order to get the same high, we need ever-higher levels . . . the television industry has gained its market share through an addictive and toxic ingredient."

"Yet, despite the mountains of research, the consensus of the medical community, and a growing list of casualties from copy-cat crimes, Hollywood continues to produce increasingly graphic and gory entertainment products, all the while denying any culpability for the violent behaviors their products inspire."

"Popular entertainment came under intense scrutiny after the tragic April 1999 massacre at Columbine High School, as published reports pointing to the Columbine killers' fondness for first-person-shooter video games and the eerie similarities between the murders and certain violent films began to emerge. There were a handful of media mea culpas as some in the entertainment industry grudgingly conceded that there might be a lose connection to violent entertainment products. Even CBS President Leslie Moonves conceded "anyone who thinks the media has nothing to do with [the bloodshed at Columbine] is an idiot."

"But has anything really changed? Is television today any less violent than it was in 1999? In the past couple of years, attention to this issue all but disappeared as our national consciousness has, understandably, turned to external threats. Has Hollywood taken advantage of this paradigm shift to start reintroducing violent content to prime time network television?"

II. Study Parameters and Methodology
"PTC analysts examined all prime time entertainment series on the major broadcast television networks (ABC, CBS, Fox, NBC, UPN and the WB) from the first two weeks of the 1998, 2000, and 2002 November sweeps periods. The ITV network was not included in this analysis because the network was launched just a few months before the first study period and had limited original programming in 1998 and 2000. A total of 400 program hours were analyzed."

"Television broadcasts of movies, news, and sports programs were not included in this analysis."

"PTC analysts reviewed the programs for all instances of violence. Mild forms of violence included threats of violence, mayhem or pyrotechnics (fires, explosions, car crashes), deaths implied, and fist fights or martial arts fights. More extreme examples of violence included use of guns or other weapons, depiction of blood, graphic depictions (e.g. a dismembered body), deaths depicted, and torture."

III. Statistical Overview

- *Overall, violence increased in every time slot between 1998 and 2002. On all the networks combined, violence was 41% more frequent during the 8:00 p.m. (ET/PT) Family Hour in 2002 than in 1998.*

- *UPN and Fox had the highest rate of violence during the Family Hour in 2002, with 7.5 and 4.67 instances per hour respectively. ABC had the largest percentage increase during the Family Hour, going from .13 instances per hour in 1998 to 2 instances per hour in 2002 (an increase of more than 1400%).*

- *The WB and CBS had the least violence, both in terms of absolute numbers and per-hour rates during the Family Hour in 2002, with .11 and .21 instances per hour respectively.*

- *CBS and the WB were also the only networks to show any improvement during the Family Hour. CBS reduced Family Hour violence by 73.4%, going from a rate of .79 instances of violence per hour in 1998 to .21 instances per hour in 2002. The WB network went from 2.5 instances of violence per hour during the Family Hour in 1998 to 2.08 instances per hour in 2000, to .11 instances per hour in 2002. Overall, WB showed a 95.6% decrease in violence from 1998 to 2002. That drop can be attributed almost entirely to the fact that Buffy the Vampire Slayer moved from the WB network to UPN in 2001.*

- *During the second hour of prime time (9-10:00 p.m. ET/ PT), violence was 134.4% more frequent in 2002 than in 1998. During the third hour of prime time (10-11:00 p.m. ET/PT) violent content was nearly 63% more common in 2002 than in 1999.*

- *Violent content was found to become more common in later hours of prime time. Violence was 149% more frequent during the second hour of prime time than during the Family Hour in 2002. Fights were 16% more common; graphic depictions increased in frequency from .02 instances per hour during the Family Hour to .54 instances per hour during the 9:00 p.m. (ET/PT) time slot; and depictions of death increased from .13 instances per hour to .87 during the second hour of prime time.*

- *The WB, UPN, and CBS had the highest per-hour rates for violence during the second hour of prime time. On the WB, violence spiked from an average of 1 instance per hour in 1998 to 6.7 instances per hour in 2002 (an increase of 570%). UPN had the largest increase, going from .13 instances per hour in 1998 to 6.6 instances per hour in 2002 (an increase of nearly 5,000%). CBS had the smallest increase, with 5 instances per hour in 1998 and 6.5 instances of violence per hour in 2002 for an increase of 30%. NBC was the only network to improve during the second hour of prime time, going from 3.14 instances of violence per hour in 1998 to 1.33 instances per hour in 2002 for a decrease of 57.6%.*

- *Only three broadcast networks continue their program feed into the 10:00 hour: ABC, CBS, and NBC. All three of those networks showed a small increase in depictions of violence during that hour from 1998 to 2002. ABC aired 27% more violence in 2002; CBS aired 37.8% more violence; and NBC aired 78.5% more violence in 2002 than in 1998. CBS had the highest rate of violence during the 10:00 hour in 2002 at 8.1 instances per hour. ABC had the lowest, at 3 instances per hour.*

- *In qualitative terms, television violence seemed to have become more graphic over time. In 1998 the most common form of TV violence during all hours of prime time was fist fights or martial arts fights (where no one was killed). By 2002, these relatively mild fight sequences became less frequent and were supplanted by more frequent use of guns or other weapons. In 1998, 44% of all violent scenes during the Family Hour were mild fight sequences compared to 32% in 2002. In 1998, 29% of all violent sequences included the use of guns or other weapons. By 2002, that number increased to 38%.*

Other Findings:

- *Use or depictions of blood in violent scenes were more common in the Family Hour in 2002 than in 2000 on ABC, NBC, and UPN (there were no depictions of blood within the study period in 1998 during the Family Hour). Fox had no change (with .33 instances per hour both years), and CBS and WB actually presented fewer violent scenes with blood in 2002 than in 2000.*

- *Looking at the second hour of prime time, violent scenes containing depictions of blood were 141% more common in 2002 than in 1998. ABC, CBS, Fox, and UPN all had more frequent depictions of blood during this time slot in 2002 than in 1998. NBC had 31.2% fewer depictions of blood in 2002 than in 1998.*

- *On the whole, the use of guns and other weapons in Family Hour programs increased by 85.1% between 1998 and 2002, although some individual networks did show some improvement. ABC, Fox, and UPN all had more scenes containing guns or other weapons in 2002 than in 1998, NBC, CBS, and the WB had fewer.*

- *During the second hour of prime time there was a 200% increase in scenes depicting the use of guns or other weapons between 1998 and 2002. NBC was the only network to reduce the frequency of such scenes during this time slot by 2002. CBS remained constant at 1.4 instances per hour of gun play or use of other weapons in both 1998 and 2002.*

- *The per-hour rate of deaths depicted has slowly climbed since 1998 in every time slot. During the Family Hour in*

1998, there were .06 deaths depicted per hour. By 2002, that number reached .13. During the second hour of prime time in 1998, there were .35 deaths depicted per hour. By 2002, it had increased to .87. During the 10:00 p.m. (ET/PT) time slot, deaths depicted per hour rose from .23 to 1.7.

©©©
Dollars and cents . . .
Is that what we're about?
Doesn't make sense . . .
Why are we falling out?
©©©
Letting things go . . .
Not giving a damn.
Just goes to show . . .
That society's a sham.
©©©
Our kids are going crazy . . .
As we stand idly by.
Getting fat and real lazy . . .
And you wanna know why?
©©©
Just look around you . . .
At the world we live in.
Who you trying to fool . . .
While you're living in sin?
©©©
Doing the things . . .
And following the path,
That money brings.
Gee that's so sad . . .
©©©
But what can one do?
In a world so lost.
You know that it's true . . .
What did it cost?
©©©
You tell me . . .

We sit around wondering . . . how . . . when? Where did we go wrong? Why is this happening? Why are our kids so hateful . . . so violent . . . so lost? Come on . . . get a grip! Open your eyes to the reality that is sitting right in front of you. WE ARE THE CAUSE! You and I. I know that I was part of the problem in a very big way, because I was one of those gang members pulling youngsters into the game. I was a direct participant. But every one of you were participants as well. Indirect participants by your refusal to wake up and smell the coffee . . . by your inaction . . . by your safe haven of ignorance to the problem. Maybe you don't want to hear that, but it is the truth and I am going to tell it you. Now that we have established culpability, let's do something and become part of the solution. I know that I am going to do everything in my power and through-out the rest of my life to be a part of the solution, starting with this book.

If I can talk to one kid at a time and change his path . . . his direction . . . his focus . . . then I am doing something. It doesn't have to be on a mass scale. Just one kid at a time. If all of us take the time to help just one kid at a time . . . we'll be doing big things! I'm talking to all of you ex-gang members as well, who are out of the game, but not doing anything worthwhile in your lives. Get out there. Start getting at these kids and give them the benefit of your experience in the game. Set them on the right course, and by virtue of that, you may also be set on your right course!

Just listen good to today's music . . . watch the movies that are out there with an open mind. Don't watch it as entertainment, but rather focus on its content . . . you'll be shocked. And if you aren't then maybe you need a role model as well. Go out and find you one.

None of us are paying attention to what is going on right in front of us, with our own children. We have allowed a modern day Sodom and Gomorrah to be created and we are living in total social disorder. We exist in direct contradiction of sound bible principles and will sow what we reap if we allow it to continue. It's no wonder why our world is in the toilet and why so many things are happening day after day. Is this the legacy that we want to leave our children and their children? Is it any wonder that they are experiencing so may issues? I think not!

The world is full of rampant sexually transmitted diseases because of our permissiveness to sexual immorality. We need not wonder why STD's are so pandemic. It's right in our faces. Or why teen promiscuity and pregnancy is on the rise. We know why. We just refuse to acknowledge why. Why sexual abuse of every sort is so rampant. Or even to admit that it is a problem unless it hits us on a personal level. The proof is in the pudding and we are making the pudding.

Yes indeed . . . it is truly up to you and me . . . and everyone else. We all need to stand up and take responsibility for this world and the activities occurring in it . . . the chaos that we have created . . . and the destruction that we have thrust upon our children through social deterioration. We all need to read and implement the wisest play of all. The Holy Scriptures tell us word for word how to rise up positive responsible sons and daughters. We would do well to take heed and take hold of these moral standards. If not for ourselves, then out of love and for the sake of our children, who will be left holding the bag.

Somewhere along the paths of our busy lives, the "American Dream" has supplanted the family unit. Everyone is striving to own the best house, drive the nicest car, have all the luxuries, and so on. What happened to striving for integrity, honor, and family love? What happened to personal parenting? Everyone has somewhere to go . . . somewhere to be . . . someone to see . . . etc.! We are a society on the go and that my friends, comes with a hefty price. We eat on the go and live in the fast lane. It's all about getting there first . . . beating the next man . . . being on top! But where are we going? The world is in a tailspin. It's a wreck . . . is this where we are headed? Well, have I got news for you! We are already here and it stinks! Get out of the race. It's not going anywhere. It doesn't mean anything. What will you win? What will you lose? How about your children . . . your values . . . your morality . . . and your integrity? Where do they fit in? Got no room for them? Too bad! What about your children? You got room for them? Or are they to be left by the wayside too?

Rat race
From Wikipedia, the free encyclopedia

Artist's depiction of the modern day rat race

"A rat race is a term used for an endless, self-defeating or pointless pursuit. It conjures up the image of the futile efforts of a lab rat trying to escape while running around a maze or in a wheel. In an analogy to the modern city, many rats in a single maze expend a lot of effort running around, but ultimately achieve nothing (meaningful) either collectively or individually."

"The rat race is a term often used to describe work, particularly excessive work; in general terms, if one works too much, one is in the rat race. This terminology contains implications that many people see work as a seemingly endless pursuit with little reward or purpose. Not all workers feel like that. For example, self-employment contributes to an increase in job satisfaction and the self-employed may experience less job related mental strain."

"The increased image of work as a "rat race" in modern times has led many to question their own attitudes to work and seek a better alternative; a more harmonious Work-life balance. Many believe that long work hours, unpaid overtime, stressful jobs, time spent commuting, less time for family life and/or friends life, has led to a generally unhappier workforce/population unable to enjoy the benefits of increased economic prosperity and a higher standard of living."

Escaping the rat race can have a number of different meanings:

- *A description of the movement, of either the Home or Work Location, of previously City Dwellers or Workers to more rural locations*
- *Retirement in general or no longer needing / having to work.*
- *Moving from a high pressure job to a less intense role either at a different company or within the same company at an alternative location or department.*
- *Changing to a different job that does not involve working 9 to 6 and a long commute.*
- *Working from home.*
- *Becoming financially independent from an employer.*

"A rat race is a fierce competition to maintain or improve one's position in the workplace or social life. This term presumably alludes to the rat's desperate struggle for survival. [Colloquial; first half of 1900s]"

"Urban planners often use the term 'rat racing' to describe behavior by motorists who choose to travel to the most direct route by using secondary roads not intended for through traffic."
http://en.wikipedia.org/wiki/Rat_race

You can rest assured that they will "Get in where they fit in" and that is the truth. So, if you don't make room for them, you can bet that the gangs certainly will. Are you willing to sacrifice them for the sake of success? Success, what does that really mean? Are your children the cost of selling your soul to life on the go? Does money make up for all that is lost? Can you put a price on love, on morals, or on principles?

Who do your children interact with when you are too busy to do so? With one another? With the thugs on the block? Do you even know? Do you even care? Have you asked them? Come on folks! Wake up and snap out of it! It's time for reform . . . personal reform . . . not the reform the politicians talk about . . . that's garbage . . . I'm talking real reform . . . within the family unit. Let's quit stalling and start overhauling . . . making changes.

Doing what's right to make a better, brighter, and more positive future for our children and their children. It's really up to us and we need to get a grip and a move on. We must eliminate the threat of gangs before they overrun us. We can do this with education and family values. Let's end hatred with Christian love and morality. Let's invest in their future and deliver them. Let's give them a fighting chance and put a stop to the senseless disregard for life and the proliferation of gang activity.

Let's quit tossing our values away for the sake of success and expediency. It is up to us as individual parents to instill the values needed for our children's successful transition into early adulthood. It isn't self-taught. Let's get involved with area schools and help those who teach our young to instill good principles. Let's help the next generation to rise to another level of humanity, integrity, and morality.

Let's not stand idly by as they descend into the depths on inhumanity because of ignorance and isolation. It's what we do . . . ignore and isolate. Don't pass the buck . . . instead carry your load. Educators can only do so much. We must step in and lend a helping hand and give moral support. The school system alone cannot carry the burden that should be picked up at home. Let's change the laws that tie the hands of parents and educators to teach our children with disciplined temperance. By doing so we take the war zone out of the schools and replace it with order.

We are too busy . . . we pay our taxes . . . don't we? We have car payments we have to make, boat payments that are due, and home payments too. We don't have time for this? Is that really fair? Who bears the cost? Who loses? Our children do!

©©©
It's a rat race . . .
A hectic pace.
I run around . . .
Trying to gain ground.
©©©
Fast and in a hurry . . .
The rest is all blurry.
Missing out on livin' . . .
Forget about the givin',

©©©
Gotta get my piece . . .
Condo on a lease.
Driving my brand new car . . .
Trying to reach the stars.
©©©
How about you?
Whatta you do?
Whatta you drive?
Living in a dive?
©©©
I gotta brand new spot.
My cars hella hot.
But what did it cost me?
The loss of my family!

How to discourage your children from joining gangs

Discourage your children from hanging around with gang members. Talk to them about it. Let them know your concerns. Meet your children's friends. Find out who they are, what influence they have on your children and how they and your children spend their free time. Listen to them when they interact around you. Listen to their language and their tone. If your children choose friends that are mostly from gangs, then your children are probably involved or will become involved in one also.

Occupy your children's free time. Give them responsibilities at home. Get them involved in after-school sports, city/county recreation, dance, the arts, and other busy activities. Be interested in your child's daily affairs. Let them know that you are paying attention and want to be involved. Praise them for doing well.

Develop good communication with your children. Good communication is open and frequent, and it takes on a positive tone. Be understanding yet firm. It allows your children to come to you to discuss any topic or problem. Do not condemn them or put them down. Listen and offer positive sound solutions. Don't scream and yell at them, they are not trying to hear all of that. That type of action closes the door to good communication rather quickly. Good communication allows you to tell your children that you love them.

Spend time with your children. Plan activities that the whole family can enjoy. Spend time alone with your children. Expose them to different places outside of your neighborhood: parks, museums, the beach, the mountains, camping trips, etc. Just have a conversation with your child for the sake of conversing. Let them feel that they are being acknowledged.

Do not buy or allow your children to dress in gang style clothing. Be proactive. Learn about gang and drug activity in your community. Learn how gang members dress, how they speak, their behavior and their activities. Attend information meetings, read articles related to gang activity. If your children dress in gang style clothing, they are expressing an interest in gangs and will attract the attention of gangs. If they are in the wrong neighborhood at the wrong time, they could be victimized or killed. Do not allow your children to write or practice writing gang names, symbols, or any other gang graffiti on their books, papers, clothes, bodies, walls or any other place.

Set limits for your children. At an early age, children need to know what is acceptable and what is unacceptable behavior. Do not allow your children to stay out late or spend a lot of unsupervised time out in the streets.

Teach them respect for others' property. Develop an anti-gang environment in your home. Clearly and continually begin to express to your children at an early age your disapproval of gang activity and of any family members joining a gang. Be an informed parent.

In closing I would just like to urge all parents, siblings, aunts, uncles, and grandparents to take a little time out of each of your lives and reach out to a kid who is at risk and show him that there are choices in life, that they are not alone, and that they do not have to choose gangs for acceptance and as a way of life. Let's do the right thing! Be a role model to somebody!

Manuel Jaramillo